Data without Drama

Navigating
Critical Thinking, Communication, and Ethics in the Age of AI

Zacharias Voulgaris and Daniel Angermann

Technics Publications
SEDONA, ARIZONA

TECHNICS PUBLICATIONS

115 Linda Vista, Sedona, AZ 86336 USA

https://www.TechnicsPub.com

Edited by Steve Hoberman

Cover design by Lorena Molinari

First Printing 2026

ISBN, print ed. 9798898160852
ISBN, Kindle ed. 9798898160869
ISBN, PDF ed. 9798898160876

Library of Congress Control Number: 2026938240

Contents

Introduction

"75% of long-term job success depends on people skills, while only 25% on technical knowledge."

Peggy Klaus

A tale of two data professionals

Let's start with a story in the world of data work, one involving two data professionals: Chris Thomas and John Dorian. Both are in the same role, but in different departments of the same company. Their daily work involves handling data from various sources, organizing data pipelines, working with complex models (mostly AI-based), and providing useful insights and, sometimes, data products to their supervisors.

Naturally, both of these data professionals know their stuff and have plenty of experience in their fields. However, they differ in a few key ways: Chris is mature in critical thinking, communication, and ethical action, while John is a novice in these areas.

As is often the case, the data they deal with is riddled with biases and various problems. The different people they work with have vastly different backgrounds and their understanding of data varies greatly. Since much of the data involves Personally Identifiable Information (PII), extra care is needed when handling it, but the organization has no clear guidelines. Due to their roles, Chris and John have to address these challenges effectively, as the company aspires to be data-driven, given the high stakes for the products involved.

John Dorian tackles these challenges more linearly, focusing on the more quantifiable aspects rather than on the methods and processes of data work. Generally, he either delegates or escalates the problems he can't solve himself. Communication is kept formal and polite, without engaging in anything beyond what's expected. After all, he's very busy with other, more important tasks. As a result, he doesn't get reprimanded often, but he doesn't have many prospects for any kind of career advancement in the next five years.

On top of that, he often gets frustrated and upset, especially when communicating with his teammates, and generally brings down the whole team when he fails to handle problems (due to his lack of critical thinking). Additionally, he often makes dubious decisions regarding the use of sensitive data (lack of ethics), making him even less likable to those who take notice. As a result of all this, his supervisors are certain that in the next downsizing, he will be among those let go.

Chris Thomas, on the other hand, has a more systematic approach to tackling these challenges. He addresses them more objectively, thanks to his critical thinking, and isn't shy about communicating with everyone else involved in a mutually beneficial way. He's great at engaging his audience, thanks to his communication ability and making them feel more like stakeholders rather than passive recipients of what he has to say. He enjoys working by himself, too, but whether he's tackling the design of a new pipeline, a script, or a dashboard, he always keeps the end user in mind and makes sure a faulty model discriminates against no one. He tends to feel challenged, not by others but by himself, because of the standards he has and his aspiration to constantly get better at his craft. His promotion review is coming up next quarter.

Today, the drama of the processes and cultures around data makes data work more challenging. Although it's hard to find two data professionals who are identical in everything except these specific aptitudes, the morale of the story remains relevant today. This is particularly the case as AI becomes increasingly adept at hard skills and technical knowledge, which have been the key differentiators of information workers until now.

The trifecta of thinking, communicating, and acting ethically

Thinking (critically), communicating, and acting ethically are the trifecta for data work that we focus on in this book. These qualities are a surefire way to help us transcend the drama and focus on the data aspects of our work. They were not selected randomly, as they constitute the three pillars of being an effective data professional, especially today. But what does this trifecta entail exactly?

First of all, it's all about thinking more critically and developing the mental discipline to make meaningful, fact-driven decisions. This may not sound like something new, but its relevance remains and even grows as we outsource more and more of our thinking and our critical faculties to advanced cognitive systems. If we could get by with basic thinking skills in the past, that's not the case anymore, in the era of AI agents. Critical thinking adds value to all kinds of data processes. It helps us tackle plenty of problems (more on that later), come up with viable solutions, and build confidence in the face of data-related adversity.

At a time when many people put their minds (and their lives) on autopilot, trusting large language models (LLMs) for more and more decisions, we advocate the opposite, without neglecting the positive use cases of such systems.

The trifecta also encompasses communicating effectively and with a purpose that benefits everyone involved. It's all about constructive storytelling and information exchange, fostering understanding and better collaboration. The communication we talk about is free of rhetorical tricks and power games, and it is geared toward aligning goals and values, something that AI systems still fail to achieve, no matter how large their context windows grow. We view and strive for communication that brings everyone on the same page, encourages them to contribute, and incorporates their input. It's a communication that builds on critical thinking rather than acting skills, full of meaningful questions that help us understand different points of view and address them properly.

Moreover, incorporating ethics into every action and the aforementioned processes is another aspect of the trifecta. Even though many people talk about ethics in data work as more of an afterthought or something specialists would only bother with, we bring it to a more prominent place in the data work process. Ethics and action based on it are more than just something we include to appear virtuous or to silence various critics; they're an integral part of everything we advocate. That's why we cover it across various parts of the book and showcase it in all kinds of scenarios that reflect the nuances of data work today. Ethics is essential to every data professional's work, regardless of whether specialized committees are in place. And it's more than just philosophizing about what's right or wrong, but about driving actions through balanced decisions that no one will regret in the next quarter or year.

Furthermore, the trifecta is related to ensuring that we are not emotionally bound to our work with data. This emotional attachment is often the root of the drama that arises in data projects, leading people to become overly defensive and rigid. However, this isn't conducive to progress and often leads to problems of all sorts, from dysfunctional collaboration to lack of objectivity. Critical thinking, proper communication, and ethical action tackle this issue head-on and help us stay non-attached to data work, all while giving it our best (i.e., we aren't indifferent to the results of our projects).

Finally, the trifecta also involves developing a mindset and culture based on these principles and applying them to data work. It's much more than a checklist or something to get excited about until finishing reading a book or until you need to "get back to work." Thinking, speaking, and acting as proposed in this book is a way to shape one's reality and form habits around it. If done properly, it's also a way to evolve as a data professional and deliver value that no machine is capable of yet.

About the book

This book tackles various problems often encountered in data work that may even hinder the most well-planned data initiatives. These include, but are not limited to, the following:

AI-related:

- Dependency on AI and experts for critical analyses and decisions
- The Illusion of Objectivity
- The "Black Box" Problem of Complex Models
- Ethical Debt in AI Systems

Communication- and collaboration-related:

- Miscommunications and issues with collaboration
- Communicating Uncertainty and False Positives
- Accountability Dilution in the Data Pipeline (tackling this enables better growth in data professionals)
- Incoherence in the (data) culture of the organization

Ethics- and strategy-related:

- Biases and ethical pitfalls (directly related to the issue of the scalability of harm)
- Sub-optimal strategies for tackling complex data problems
- Data Privacy versus Utility
- Value-Sensitive Design and "Solutions in Search of a Problem"

Although, for the sake of simplicity, we won't go through all of them in detail, suffice to say that they tend to creep up in various projects, especially those involving advanced models (mostly AI-based), sensitive or complex data, and people at various levels of data literacy. Instead of focusing on specific scenarios, we focus on general approaches to problems across these verticals. Otherwise, it's easy to fall into the trap of over-optimizing for this or the other issue and lose sight of the bigger picture. Nevertheless, throughout the book, we provide specific scenarios in which one or more of these problems appear, and we demonstrate how they are tackled using one or more aspects of the Critical Thinking, Communication, and Ethics (think, speak, act) trifecta.

The book is structured as follows. First, we start with an overview and description of the problem, examining the whys and hows of the trifecta (Chapters 1 and 2, respectively). We'll focus on critical thinking and communication, as ethical action is usually implied. Then, we'll look at how the whole thing works in practice (Chapter 3), with specific examples.

The middle of the book will delve into specific frameworks of each aspect of the trifecta. Again, we'll focus on critical thinking (Chapter 4) and communication (Chapter 6), as they are the parts that require more hands-on work and explanation, while ethics is covered in these chapters anyway. Nevertheless, we'll also have a dedicated chapter (5) where we'll look into some ethics-specific ideas.

The next part of the book is all about the trifecta's relationship with AI (Chapter 7) and the steps you can take to better assimilate all these ideas, along with some concluding remarks (Chapter 8). There, we'll look into the data culture aspects of the organization, too, as well as the general benefits of this trifecta in society. Besides, ideas like the ones we put forward in this book are meant to be shared and applied at a larger scale. That's when they are best validated and offer the most value, anyway.

Throughout the book, we'll have various case studies to illustrate the points made in each chapter. Naturally, the real value of all this knowledge and know-how will come when you apply it to your own situations and specific data-related problems you face in your day-to-day work. Additionally, each main chapter will include a list of key takeaways to help retain its most important points.

In an effort to keep this book short and to the point, we refrain from including any appendices. This is why we opted for an accompanying website for this book (https://data-without-drama.carrd.co), where we will include additional resources and quizzes to keep these ideas fresh and easier to share with your colleagues. Additionally, we encourage you to discuss the ideas presented in this book, how they apply to our lives, and share any relevant insights with others.

So, without any further ado, let's get started!

CHAPTER 1

Critical Thinking and Communication 101

"It is the mark of an educated mind to be able to entertain a thought without accepting it."

Aristotle

Let's establish a common understanding of the abstract concepts of critical thinking and communication and how they apply in the current world. We will take a look at the central mental models we consider and their application. By the end of this section, you will have a grasp of what these terms mean, which common models can be used, and how these concepts apply to modern data work.

The process we aim for starts with proper analysis through critical thinking and subsequent communication.

Critical thinking

Critical thinking has been defined as "the purposeful, self-regulatory judgment which results in interpretation, analysis, evaluation, and inference, as well as explanation of the evidential, conceptual, methodological, criteriological, or contextual considerations upon which that judgment is based."[1]

The American Philosophical Association coined this definition in 1990, and it fits its original audience: philosophers. In the following paragraphs, we will examine this definition and more recent interpretations to create a definition for everyday use. The goal, however, remains the same: solving problems.

In the traditional process, we can break the lengthy description of critical thinking down into multiple parts.

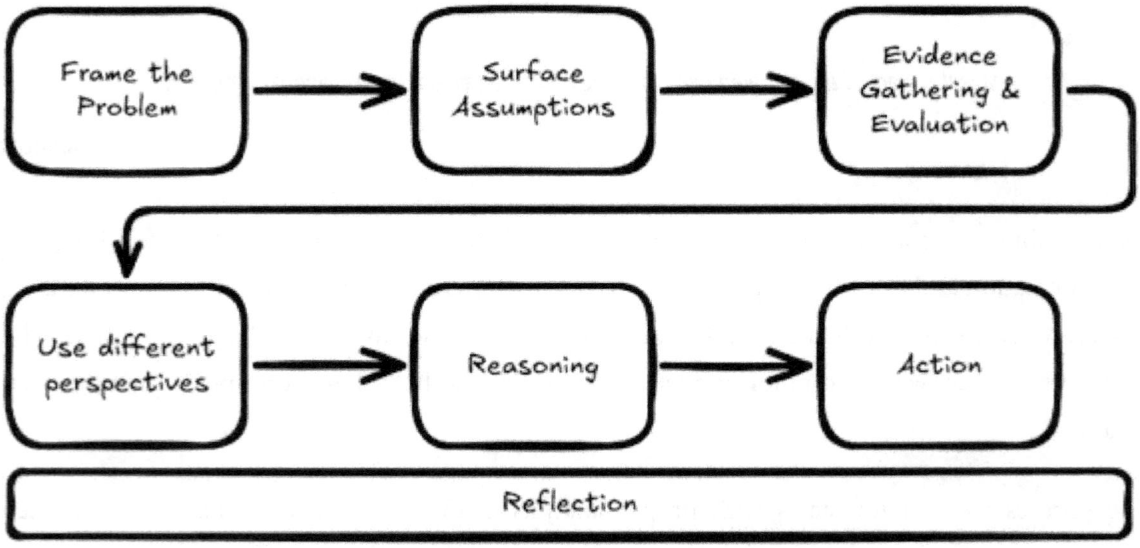

Figure 1: Steps of the traditional critical thinking process.

The "judgment" requires an answer to a question or hypothesis. This question needs to be well-formed and, ideally, consist of testable claims. This is often called "Framing the Problem". We cannot start solving a problem until we fully understand it and define how to evaluate it. This includes us defining the steps to follow after a decision.

[1]Facione, Peter A., Critical Thinking: A Statement of Expert Consensus for Purposes of Educational Assessment and Instruction. Research Findings and Recommendations." 1990.

Let's look at an example to illustrate this important first step. Our example is "Should we roll out new product X?" This is a binary question, meaning it has only two answers: yes or no. Which means it is not in itself measurable. But there are implicit claims in there which we need to make explicit. Possible claims could be: "Product X will open new market A to us," or "Product X will successfully replace the inferior Product W," or even both. Real-life problems often involve multiple claims, defined by the various functions in your organization. Sales may project different expectations on the new product than your engineering department. Still, those claims are not measurable yet they lead us to the success criteria. For "Product X will open new market A to us," it could be "x amount of new revenue in market A in Q3." An initial binary question has become a measurable outcome. On the way, the implied goals have been surfaced.

A base check for this phase can be a framing along the following format:

"We will decide [decision] by [measure] to achieve [claim]; success looks like [value X]."

The next step in the process is to identify the assumptions underlying the claims. Or consider the constraints under which the decision has to be made. As in the first step, none of this will be surprising or new, but it needs to make its way from the collective unconscious to the public. Otherwise, the implications of the earlier outcomes may be lost.

Let's explore from our previous example, the claim "Product X will open new market A to us." A base assumption contained within that is that "the organization is not yet active within market A," which needs to be checked. If the organization is (so far unknowingly) active in this market, it can have implications for launching another product in the same market, cannibalization, or synergies. Another assumption is that the entry into market A is generally beneficial to the organization. This sounds simple, but it can have massive consequences if there is no Product-Market fit or if the markets one already serves react badly to the entry.

Again, a single sentence can be used as a guideline:

"This holds only if [assumption]; we'd be wrong if [inverse assumption]."

With the problem well-defined and our assumptions about it documented, we can proceed to the gathering and evaluation of evidence. Evidence can be data in its many forms, as well as expert opinions or other forms of input. Challenges can include the unavailability of input for innovations or the presence of too much evidence for well-covered topics. The first can be covered by personal experimentation or exploration, which is the most genuine form of evidence-gathering. The latter should be mitigated by the explicit claims and required measures outlined in the problem framing. Additionally, each piece of evidence needs to be evaluated according to its provenance, recency, and representativeness. The overall quality needs to fit the purpose of the analysis.

Biased data, anecdotes, or unrelated evidence will prevent proper analysis.

In our example of rolling out Product X, evidence could include existing market research, user interviews, or active experimentation, such as a very limited rollout followed by a subsequent evaluation.

As soon as the conclusions from the evidence arrive, we start drafting competing explanations. Central questions to create those are "What else could cause this?" or "What would change the conclusion?" So we are looking for weaknesses in the conclusion by taking on a contrarian role. This can be done via *Steelmanning*, creating and addressing the strongest counterargument to the current result. The name of this practice stems from the straw man fallacy in which an argument outside the current discussion is refuted without acknowledging this distinction.

Returning to our example of a possible launch of Product X, we could identify external factors that would support successful experiments, such as unique circumstances that encourage sales.

With the different perspectives taken, we can now construct the conclusion, the recommendation, or the concrete decision to the initial problem. The statements we created for the framing of the problem and the assumptions can now be validated. In case of remaining uncertainties, expected ranges or scenarios can be generated as an outcome.

Based on the recommendation, the appropriate action or actions must now be executed. We defined these activities while framing the problem.

Besides the process outlined above, other factors also determine the quality of the judgment.

Underlying the entire process is a reflection and learning practice that requires us to constantly check our approach as we explore answers. This practice, usually called *metacognition*, involves monitoring and regulating our own thinking, weighing evidence and the quality of our processes, and acknowledging our individual limits.

This can be done by evaluating how we implemented the different steps of the process and whether and how changes to those methods would have affected the individual outcomes. Anything we discover should be used immediately in the current process, if possible, or at least in future iterations.

Another factor is the disposition of the person performing the decision-making. Ideally, we cultivate a culture of inquisitiveness, open-mindedness, fair-minded evaluation, truth-seeking, and willingness to reconsider. These all amount to a state of complete neutrality regarding the initial question and the findings along the way. It also describes full trust in the process and, therefore, following it step by step. Shortcuts, like skipping steps considered unnecessary, will always impair the outcome.

One common assumption regarding the concept of critical thinking is that it requires a high level of intelligence. But, as just shown, diligently following a linear process and maintaining general open-mindedness are all that is required. Smart people can and will do dumb things when dispositions and meta-cognition are weak.

Although the terms are often used synonymously, critical thinking is not the same as analytical thinking. Analytical thinking involves breaking complex problems into smaller ones and analyzing them systematically. In analyzing those smaller questions, one then applies the critical thinking we have defined above.

We promised a shortened version of the initial definition:

Critical thinking is the disciplined, objective appraisal of information that leads to well-grounded decisions.

Communication

Very broadly defined, communication is the purposeful transmission of information. Communication is considered a key aspect of the success of the human race, as it allows the building of relationships, coordination in groups, and the sharing of knowledge.

All of those aspects have become emphasized with the rise of information technology, which gave birth to the Information Age around the mid-20th century. Today, you will find it hard to encounter elements of human life untouched by the central tools of this new age, the computer and the internet.

One of the most well-known models within communication theory is the Shannon-Weaver model, which we will use to provide a mental model for approaching communication. However, this model has shortcomings, including the missing feedback loop, the question of context, and the possible asymmetry of information. But the model provides easy access to communication as an abstract concept and remains valid. What may be surprising is that communication models do not care about the truth of the message, but only about its delivery.

The Shannon-Weaver model considers five components of communication: a source, transmitter, channel, receiver, and destination (as shown in the following graph). The source generates a message which the transmitter translates (or encodes) into a signal. This signal is sent through a channel, possibly influenced by noise, and decoded by a receiver for the final destination (Figure 2).

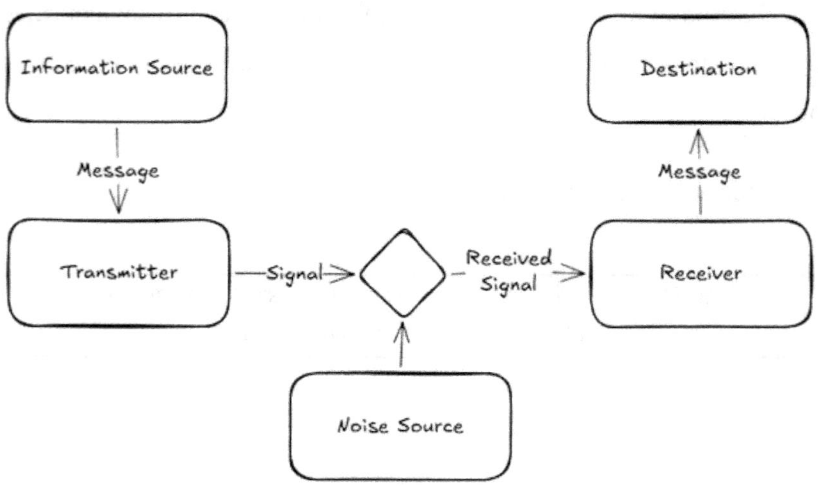

Figure 2: Communication Model according to Shannon.

Let us look at two examples to get a handle on this model: a face-to-face conversation and an email.

In a face-to-face conversation, the person speaking is the source, the mouth is the transmitter, the air is the channel through which the sound waves travel, the listener is the destination, and the ear is the receiver. Possible noise could be wind or other conversations occurring at the same time and place.

In an email, the person writing the email is the source, the computer or email program is the transmitter, the internet is the channel, another email program is the receiver, and the person reading the email is the destination. One could add more layers regarding the transmitter, channel, and receiver as the signal travels through the layers of software and hardware. This multiple encoding and decoding is part of the model and can be used to examine different levels of granularity. The most curious aspect of this is the repeated occurrence of noise at every level.

As these examples show, this model can be applied to various, if not all, forms of communication. Consider your latest presentation, your company chat, or the latest images from your marketing campaign, and how the model components fit with them. What is the message, what is the medium? Especially in the marketing campaign, the actual medium used (print, TV,...) can influence the initial message, as Marshall McLuhan stated in "The medium is the message."[2]

But there are caveats. For instance, parallel communication happens. The verbal channel may transmit the message "The project is on track", while the non-verbal cues signal insincerity at the same time. So now, as the receiver, we have to decode this mix of signals (or noise) to achieve understanding.

Misunderstanding is the failure to transmit the initial message. This failure can occur on either side, or even both sides, of the transfer. Remember your last phone call in an area with spotty reception, or a poorly worded email from you or someone else.

Any communication can be affected by noise. While this noise can be actual acoustical noise when talking to another person, it can take any form that somehow impairs the channel or the receiver. An overflowing inbox, electromagnetic interference, or psychological factors can all be noise that

---

[2]M. McLuhan "Understanding Media: The Extensions of Man", 1964.

blocks or weakens communication. For every type, there are precautions to reduce noise. We can, for example, use spam filters in the inbox. But there are limits to every one of those tools. So another option to overcome the noise is to strengthen the initial signal from the transmitter, for example, by repeating it. We could resend the initial email in our inbox example.

Another aspect to consider is that every communication entails an active part and a passive part: sending and receiving. Only one of those sides is under our control, especially in human interactions. Even if the message is known beforehand, there is noise, and the channel is familiar to both sides, misunderstanding can still occur.

A central influence, which science also acknowledges, is the context within which the messages were transferred. Context here refers to the personal relationship, based on the (non-)existence of prior interactions between the source and the destination. Consider how much you trust the words of a lifelong friend versus those of a stranger proclaiming their truths at a street corner. Prior interactions or experiences can also shape the message itself, in the form of established tendencies that may agree or disagree with its content, regardless of their validity. This trustworthiness brings us back to the skill of critical thinking. Can we (re-)consider the legitimacy of a message or source independent of prior communication?

We already touched upon the different forms of communication but want to make them explicit for the most relevant transmission system: humans. Communication between humans can take the following forms:

- **Verbal**. The spoken word, used in conversations or speeches.
- **Non-verbal**. Body language, facial expressions, and the tone of voice used.
- **Visual**. Images, charts, videos, signs, and also emojis.
- **Written**. The written word, any text using symbols or letters.

All of these can be found in digital form nowadays. A single social media post, as well as the average business presentation, will incorporate all of those forms. This parallelization, as mentioned earlier, can enrich the delivery or disrupt it if the content of the different forms does not align.

It seems that communication faces many challenges, but you can probably tell from personal experience that it works more often than not. This is also shown by the rate of innovation and growth that we, as a human race, have achieved in ever-shortening cycles. Large-scale projects like the first Moon Landing involved up to 400,000 people who all had to be aligned in their efforts. And regarding the shortening innovation cycles, this particular project, Apollo 11, happened only 66 years after the first human flight.

Real-world value

If we are capable of examining reality truthfully and are equally skilled in communicating our insights, we can become unstoppable.

Both skills are highly transferable across roles, tech stacks, and industries, and their use extends into private life as well. Employers across industries consistently rate them among the most important predictors of workplace readiness and career progression.

Regardless of whether you are an intern, a CEO, or somebody's partner, being able to communicate your ideas clearly and in ways that engage your listeners increases the likelihood that others will accept them.

Within a professional environment, communication skills can provide the following benefits:

- **Improved productivity**. By providing clear instructions and goals, we can prevent errors caused by misunderstanding, leading to a more efficient workflow.
- **Improved conflict resolution.** Strong communication skills allow all parties to express their viewpoints, helping find common ground and resolve conflicts before they escalate.
- **Stronger relationships.** Open and clear communication fosters transparency and honesty, helping build trust and deepen understanding between individuals, both personally and professionally.
- **Boost engagement and morale.** When people feel heard and their concerns are addressed, their engagement increases and a more positive work environment is created. This is a compounding effect of the psychological safety created by the previous points.

- **Improved decision making and problem solving.** Critical thinking helps to weigh options, evaluate consequences, and make choices based on reason and evidence.
- **Increased adaptability.** Critical thinkers are more willing to consider new perspectives and adapt to challenges with flexibility.
- **Improved self-awareness.** The process encourages self-reflection, which helps to recognize biases and assumptions.

Some professional roles focus exclusively on these skills. For instance, a Public Relations (PR) person will put all their effort into communicating effectively as their role directly shapes everyone's perception of the organization, person, or cause they represent. Equally, any researcher will be laser-focused on critical thinking, as their work will eventually be challenged via peer review and any lapse will be known.

Used together, critical thinking and communication create compounding effects. Expressing one's reasoning (aloud or in writing) exposes assumptions, invites counter-evidence, and refines judgment, which in turn makes subsequent communication clearer and more persuasive.

Timeless skills

While technology and business cycles change, cognitive pitfalls and the challenges of coordination and agreement do not. As shown, critical thinking is about making decisions and ultimately solving problems. This is done by structuring uncertainty, clarifying goals, mapping assumptions, checking evidence, and potentially updating held beliefs along the way. This is a process that works in any context regardless of the tools involved. All we need is our brain and trust in the process.

The same is true for communication. Whether we work on a construction site, take part in a marketing video call, write documentation, or sit together with friends, the skill of communicating clearly and effectively will benefit us. It enables coordination, turning insights gathered via critical thinking into collective action. We create trust and remove ambiguity. We establish a shared understanding.

And even on our own, communication enables us to improve our thinking. Writing is just another form of thinking; clear prose forces us to clarify ambiguous ideas. Not just for the sake of transmitting them to others but also for us to reflect and sharpen them. Finding the right words, the nuance that feels appropriate, is what separates general rumblings from coherent and convincing ideas. As we will see later, writing is also a great starting point to improve our communication skills. If we can formulate ideas for ourselves, we can do it for others.

Unsurprisingly, data work has always been about critical thinking and communication. Its goal is to generate better decisions and improve the processes that lead to and follow them. This aligns with the goals of our two key concepts. There are differences between analytical thinking, the breaking down of complex information into manageable chunks to understand it, and critical thinking, but they support each other. When systematically collecting and examining information as part of the analysis, we should also consider its credibility and relevance. Equally, we should challenge our assumptions and biases when looking at the analytical chunks and the whole picture. Ultimately, critical thinking is a frame for analytical thinking, by evaluating the analysis itself, questioning its foundations, and considering alternative interpretations.

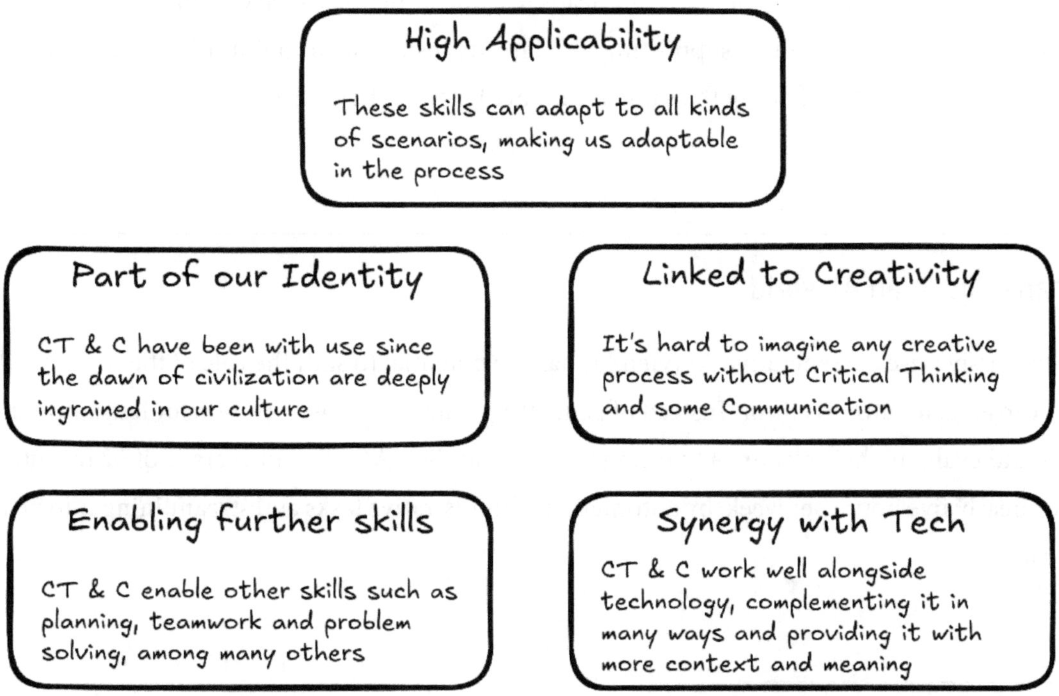

Figure 3: Critical thinking and communication (CT & T) are evergreen.

Modern work essentials

We live in worlds of increasing amounts of signals and noise. According to recent (2025) estimates, we produce over 400 exabytes of data every day.[3] Which is a number few of us can relate to. Estimates suggest that the total amount of data from all the words ever spoken by humans, if digitized, would take up roughly five exabytes. And now we generate over 80 times this per day.

This ever-growing volume and velocity of data generation bring us to the symptom of "information overload" and the increasing difficulty of separating signal from noise. The rise of misinformation, or "fake news", adds to the noise level.

Critical thinking is a tool for filtering relevant signals from noise.
Clear communication helps us make ourselves heard and rise above the noise.

Many critical thinkers fall into the trap of shortcuts in the critical thinking process, skipping the evaluation and comparison of sources and, maybe intentionally, ignoring alternative perspectives one could take with the given evidence. This leads to a phenomenon called Confirmation Bias, where one seeks out only evidence supporting an already established point of view. Professional organizations are at risk of doing the same if they are lax with their critical thinking.

Human edge in an AI world

The impressive rise of Generative AI (GenAI) has the potential to shift the role of the modern (data) worker from generator to editor. Instead of generating output, we instruct more or less autonomous agents and evaluate their results. According to recent studies, AI saves an average of 52 minutes per day, or nearly five hours per week, by automating administrative tasks and streamlining information retrieval.[4]

[3] https://my.idc.com/getdoc.jsp?containerId=US52076424

[4] https://www.forbes.com/sites/sap/2025/07/28/ai-saves-employees-5-hours-a-week---but-who-really-benefits/

But there are challenges. AI, in its chatbot form, is a constant communicator, but an unreliable one, as the phenomenon of hallucinations shows. Hallucinations are instances in which LLMs generate text that sounds correct but is factually wrong. This lies in the nature of the current technological approach, which is, at its core, a "stochastic parrot." By that, we mean a system that understands the patterns behind language and the relations among terms but does not grasp their meanings. Any LLM contains the information that "tree" and "leaf" are highly correlated, but does not grasp the abstract concept of a "tree" or the mix of feelings an autumn forest can evoke. To a degree, we can see that companies providing the LLMs shift fact-checking to us. While search engines have found ways to identify truth through rankings, this is more complex for models based on language statistics. Recent iterations of these products incorporated search capabilities to address this issue. LLMs therefore leverage the established trust of big search engines, such as Google and Bing, to provide accurate answers.

The chat interface, as a way of interacting with LLMs, tricks us to a degree. The channel (chat) makes us think the sender is similar to us, as there is no noise and the stability of the text is perceived as trustworthy. This is where critical thinking on our side becomes highly relevant. Equally, communication skills will support us in interacting with these new tools.

The main way of interacting with LLMs is through prompts, either within a chat interface or as part of a setup to build an agent consisting of multiple steps involving LLMs. Clear, structured communication has been shown to be the most effective way, as with humans, to achieve the outcomes you aim for. This *Prompt Hygiene* has many approaches, but whichever you follow should at least include your intent, the constraints you place on the problem, the success criteria, and optional guardrails for whatever solution the model provides. If this feels similar to the critical thinking process we looked at earlier, that's because it is.

But even with the perfect prompt or technical setup, we need to be wary in a time where everything can be artificially generated or manipulated. The same rigor we apply to the decision process in a professional context needs to be applied to the general world. This includes evaluating the sources we get information or news from, checking our own assumptions and biases and allowing alternative perspectives.

Real-life scenarios

Now that we know what critical thinking and communication look like, let us take a look at some recent incidents where their proper application could have prevented tragedies. Obviously, it's easy to be wise after the event, but they can still teach us what to look out for.

First, we look at the tragic crashes of the Boeing 737 MAX 8 in 2018 and 2019. A newly introduced system, Maneuvering Characteristics Augmentation System (MCAS), could trigger flight control movements without pilot intervention. The intention was to provide stabilization for the plane under certain conditions when the difference between the inflowing air and the wings is high. This system erroneously triggered multiple times based on a single external sensor and, in two cases, brought the airplanes into flight attitudes the crews could not recover from. These two crashes resulted in the death of 346 people.

According to the final report by the U.S. House Committee on Transportation and Infrastructure,[5] a lack of critical thinking and communication was central to the incidents. On the one hand, the manufacturer of the system assumed that it could operate on a single sensor input and did not challenge this assumption. While there was some consideration for a scenario in which a single sensor could provide faulty data, the respective warning system was inoperable. Tragically, the airplane model in question has two such sensors, but a reading from one was enough to trigger the system without checking the second. Equally, the manufacturer assumed that, even in the case of a mistake by the MCAS, flight crews would know what to do. This second assumption was worsened by the fact that Boeing did not communicate to the pilots the existence of MCAS and its capabilities to autonomously steer the plane.

An often-used example of large-scale corporate failure can also serve as a case for critical thinking and communication: the introduction of New Coke by the Coca-Cola Company. In April 1985, Coca-Cola launched a replacement for its original product with a new recipe and taste. But almost immediately, public backlash rose, and within only 79 days, the original beverage was reintroduced.

5 https://www.govinfo.gov/content/pkg/GOVPUB-Y4_T68_2-PURL-gpo144993/pdf/GOVPUB-Y4_T68_2-PURL-gpo144993.pdf

What is often considered a major failure in branding is also a cautionary tale about assumptions, processes, and marketing.

The company wanted to iterate on its key product, as it believed its main competitor's (Pepsi's) sweeter taste could further erode its shrinking market share. The new recipe was tested through blind-sip tests, in which participants took small sips of multiple drinks and selected their preferred drink. Within this setup, the new taste recipe won, though with some loud, concerned customer voices. Nobody challenged the validity of these sip tests compared with normal behavior, such as drinking a whole can or drinking it with food. Additional surveys showed similar patterns. But the theory of a necessary adjustment for the good of the customer was upheld. The fact that the brand and its taste had built its own identity and even traditions was not considered, and was therefore not part of the initial experimentation process.

When it came to the launch, the communication hit the wrong notes as the company spoke in product terms while the customers complained in identity terms ("Don't touch my Coke"). The company failed to connect to the consumers, missing the context.

In an age of information overload and artificial intelligence, critical thinking and communication are essential skills; they separate meaningful insight from mere noise. These capabilities empower us to navigate complexity and make sound decisions. They drive genuine progress in both our work and our lives.

Key takeaways

- Critical thinking is not about being a critic but about applying a strict process to problem solving.
- Communication is not just about sharing; it also involves considering all the factors that can interfere with the transmission of a message.
- Both skills help when interacting with humans or LLMs.

CHAPTER 2

Data Depends on the Trifecta

"It is a capital mistake to theorize before one has data."

Sherlock Holmes

Analytical work, whether as an analyst or a data scientist, requires a broad skill set. Depending on your source,[6] the skills considered essential for a data worker are the following:

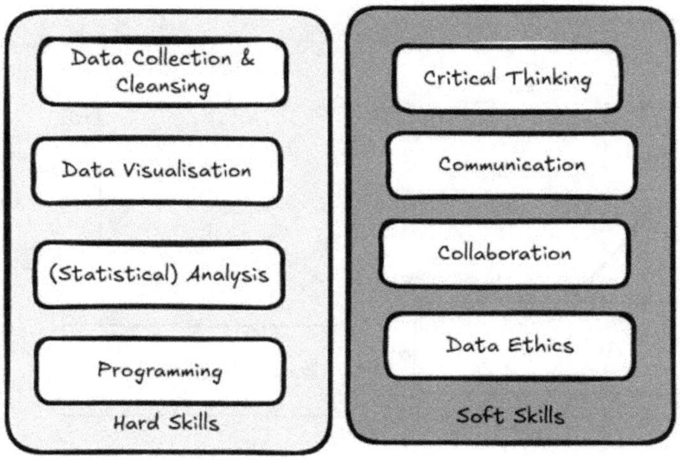

Figure 4: Key skills in data work.

6https://www.datacamp.com/blog/data-analyst-skills-for-career-success
https://graduate.northeastern.edu/knowledge-hub/data-analyst-skills/
https://advanced.jhu.edu/about/on-the-advance/mastering-your-future/10-key-skills-for-data-analysts/

And regardless of the source, you will find the two skills we have covered in the last chapter, critical thinking and communication. The latter can be hidden behind other terms like Data Storytelling or Writing Skills, but it will be ever present. Within this section, we want to look at how those two skills improve data work or work in general.

Data work as a science

Before we dive into the concrete business challenges that can be tackled, we will take a look at the primary tool for human discovery, the Scientific Method. While officially in use since the Scientific Revolution in the 16th century, the central concepts can be traced back to Ancient Greece. Within that long history, and even today, there is no fixed definition of the process but rather a general set of principles in a certain order. Those steps are:

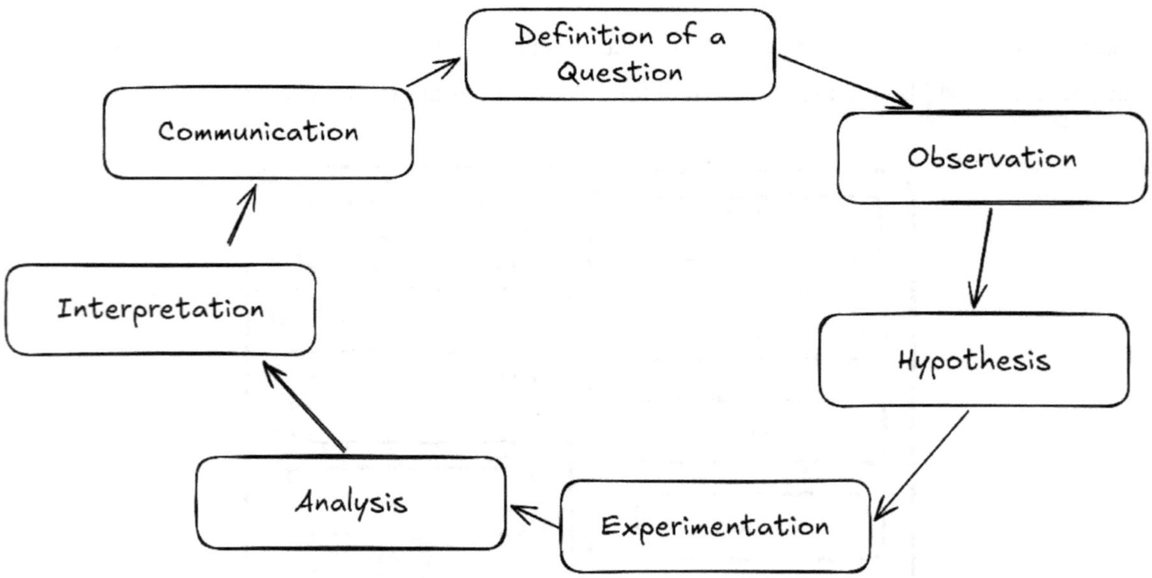

Figure 5: The Scientific Method, an iterative process.

Remembering our definition of critical thinking from Chapter 1, we see clear similarities, unsurprising given that both processes seek understanding. But they do so with different goals. The Scientific Method aims to generalize knowledge and identify core principles of how the world works. The process of critical thinking aims to support good decision making in a specific context, usually one-off. Other differences include the speed, with science often deliberately slow, and the rigor involved in observation and experimentation. In a business context, deadlines are often closer than in foundational research.

We will put the processes side by side to make their overlap clear (Figure 6).

What makes the Scientific Method relevant for data work is its combination of critical thinking and communication, as well as its iterative nature.

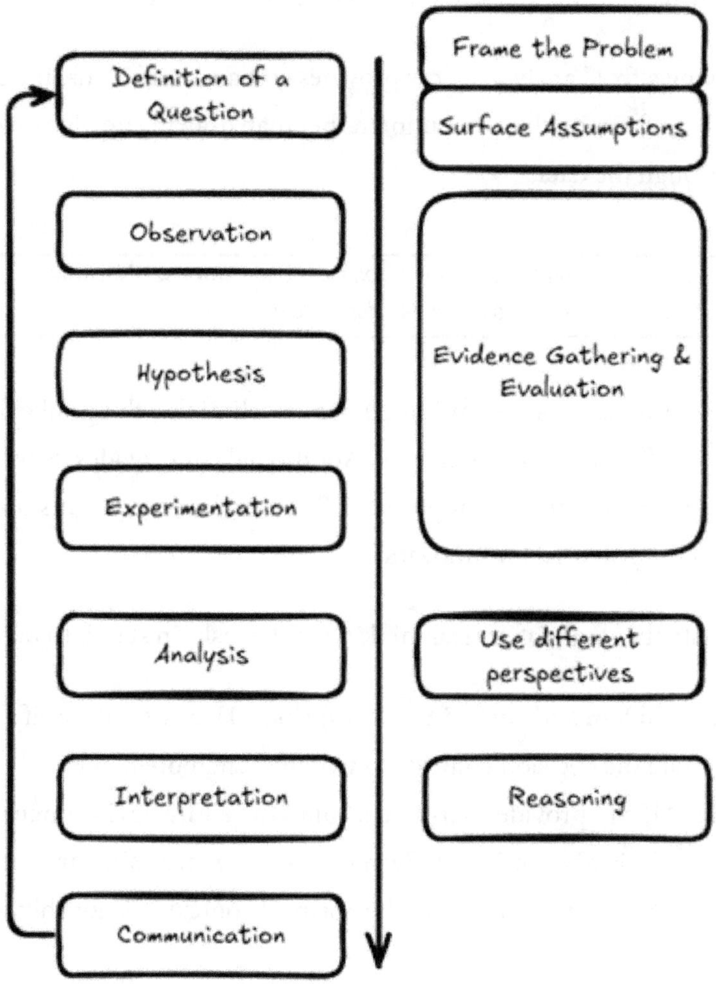

Figure 6: Comparison between the scientific method and traditional critical thinking.

The singular business decision made after analysis often raises new questions that expand on previous iterations of the cycle. Each pass builds on the last, compounding understanding and improving both the quality of our questions and the confidence in our answers.

Repetition is not a risk as long as only the broad guidelines of the process are followed and not the specifics of the last iteration. Even if the initial question or problem looks similar, or especially then. Otherwise, we run the risk of zealous analysis: proper application of the method, but a disconnect with the current business situation. As we will see below, the involvement of subject matter experts (SMEs) is essential to avoid losing track of the initial purpose or question.

Still, the rigor of having a fixed analytical flow provides guidance and focus. If we know which steps we need to cover, we can focus on their execution rather than drawing up plans every time or wasting time meandering through the data.

Critical thinking as part of the Scientific Method provides objectivity, leading to better decisions under uncertainty.

If we really follow the process, as an organization, we can eliminate things like the HiPPO (highest paid person's opinion) effect in decision making. Additionally, it provides us with openness to new influences or interpretations of the initial problem. This can lead to insights that were outside the initial scope but yield the potential for innovation.

Let us directly translate the stages of critical thinking to the tasks in standard data work:

- **Framing the problem and surfacing assumptions.** Here we will clarify the business question(s), state the decision context, constraints, and potential harms. At this stage, we will need the SMEs to provide transparency into the entire environment in which we will perform the analysis or experiment. Even if we encountered similar problems before, we should check with them to make sure the business context has not shifted.

- **Gathering evidence and evaluation.** We assess evidence quality, inherent biases, and other data quality dimensions. As there is often no definitive answer, we will need to weigh the trade-offs of using certain metrics and the costs of errors. In some cases, we will need to acknowledge that the Single Point of Truth (SPOT) does not exist. Concrete ways to evaluate data quality include the application of business rules, ideally from a central semantic layer or, at a minimum, aligned documentation.

- **Different perspectives.** When we have the first consistent results, we need to check for alternative explanations. A common practice to provide nudges towards other interpretations is to challenge the preliminary result with an uninvolved analyst or a fitting SME. This role can now also be taken over by any LLM, even if it is not trained on or provided with the relevant data or business context. The challenge alone should inspire exploration of other options.

- **Reasoning.** When it is clear that there is a causal story to share, we return to the first step and, with its input, formulate the result. Within that, we need to communicate the remaining uncertainty, either from the method itself or the evaluation of the evidence. Also, the initial assumptions and new ones we discovered during the examination will have to be shared. Ideally, our organization has a standardized approach to sharing and acting upon insights. This does not describe a PowerPoint template but rather a clear, trusted process.

- **Reflection.** Within the documentation of the analysis, which should be standard in our organization, we will look back at the challenges, technical, methodological, and maybe organizational, we encountered. And we act on the most impactful measures to address those to improve the next iteration(s). Common outcomes can include the creation of reproducibility checklists, required changes to the technical setup, or retraining data stewards regarding their responsibilities. Before the process execution, one could create a pre-mortem, a document assuming failure of the process and supporting the identification of the causes. With this knowledge, we can prevent those causes before they become effective.

In Chapter 4, we will explore this even further and find ways to apply it deliberately.

Communication gets the decisions made by humans. Or it brings clarity in the age of AI and automation about the parameters for automating decision-making, for instance, in recommendation systems or customer segmentation. The European Union, via the EU AI Act,[7] requires explainability for AI systems. It also enables stakeholders to understand how these systems work, which in turn generates buy-in for their deployment and use.

Regardless of which of those two cases we tackle, the tools are similar, if not the same. They are often summarized under the title *Data Storytelling.* The most common association is with the art of data visualization, including pie charts. But good storytelling incorporates multiple forms of communication. The write-up next to the graphs is as important as the clarity of the visuals, and is equally important as the narrative when the analysis covers a particularly complex problem.

Besides the visual and written aspects, the communication context, which is missing from the Shannon-Weaver model we looked at earlier, is key. Context is a key factor of information asymmetry, the fact that different parties, humans in our situation here, in a transaction possess unequal knowledge. A classic example is that the seller of a car knows all its faults, and the potential buyer does not. Within data work, this can refer to the data person being aware of the exact metric definitions, the quality of the sourced data, or prior analyses in the same area. This can also be the different lingo used among data and business people. Enthusiastic analysts tend to employ overly technical terms or mathematical language.

Other recent developments also influence the context. The move to remote or hybrid setups reduces opportunities for spontaneous chats or classic analysis walk-throughs. Therefore, written communication becomes more relevant. And it needs even more clarity as conversations become asynchronous. Any questions or challenges cannot be addressed immediately, which can increase the time required to transmit the information correctly.

GenAI and LLMs offer the ability to easily generate (and summarize) text, but bloat, the intentional expansion without adding actual content, or truncation can reduce the effectiveness of communication. By now, this phenomenon has become known as *workslop.*[8] This is a reference to general *AI slop*, fast-generated AI content that looks valid but is ultimately without meaning. It can be tempting to expand the three key insights or explanations into separate, great-sounding

---

7https://artificialintelligenceact.eu/

8https://hbr.org/2025/09/ai-generated-workslop-is-destroying-productivity

paragraphs. But if the recipient just feeds their LLMs the text and a prompt to distill the key insights into bullet points, a lot of unnecessary work is created, even if a machine does it.

Within Chapter 6, we will have a closer look at how to exactly practice and apply these base principles.

For easier handling, we provide the following two checklists for use with every new data project:

Communication checklist for data work:

1. What decision or behavior should this change?
2. Who needs what, in what order, with what prior knowledge?
3. What's the one message, the proof, the caveats, and the next action?
4. What uncertainties matter to the decision right now? How are we tracking them?

Critical thinking checklist for analysis:

1. What assumptions must be true? How would we know if they weren't?
2. What's the strongest rival explanation? What negates our favorite story?
3. Where could sampling, leakage, or drift invalidate this?
4. What are the stakeholder harms if we're wrong?

Common data work problems

Let us look at some common data work problems and how the application of critical thinking or great communication can solve them.

Drifting metrics

When different departments use their own revenue metric, everyone has their own definition of customer activation, or nobody knows what the acronym ARIR means anymore, we experience what is called *Semantic Drift*: a phenomenon describing the slow but steady change in a metric definition due to insignificant changes. These compound over time and lead to either a definition that no longer fits the initial purpose or, worse, to multiple parallel definitions. The toll this takes on the organization is usually a combination of mistrust, misalignment, and possibly confusion among external stakeholders such as customers, partners, and regulatory entities. Occasionally, this is called *Metric Drift*, but that term actually refers to the slow but steady shift in the value of any metric or key performance indicator (KPI) over time. It seems the definition of shift has drifted.

This is where critical thinking and communication can be the right tools for discovery and correction. If we encounter unexpected or non-matching values for our central metrics, we can consider it a data project. And with this, we can apply critical thinking, or the Scientific Method as its bigger brother. We define the problem, for instance, "Which of the revenue values is true?" and surface the underlying assumptions. The latter can be our experience with earlier valid definitions of those metrics.

Our next step is to collect evidence and to evaluate the data sources. The key questions are, "Where do these values come from, and who is responsible for them?" Also, "What purpose do they serve?" Especially the last question may lead us to accept different perspectives of the different parts of our organization. With all of this, we can conclude which definition to use. It is not uncommon for none of the encountered values to be correct with respect to the organization's current needs.

After the proper definition has been identified, we need to ensure it is applied where needed. This includes confirming that redundant or invalid definitions and uses are discontinued. Otherwise, we have just picked the right version for the current circumstances, and the zoo of metrics persists, which will lead to the same problem again. Our communication skills will help us prevent this. Using written documentation, a shared glossary, or a central metrics tree, we can launch a campaign to enforce the new rules. Why written? It provides the official channel with the least noise. Written text is still considered the more credible and more persistent source for information. As people can skim it, consume it at their own pace, and search it more easily, it remains the most accessible way to distribute knowledge. Part of that campaign is the (re-)assignment of ownership of the metric definition. In case redundant definitions were found, we also need to revoke ownership from the former owners.

Spurious correlations

We can assume everyone has heard the adage that "correlation is not causation," but things become classics for a reason. But our two tools can be effective again.

Spurious causality or correlation is the misleading observation that two variables are causally linked when that relation is coincidental or driven by an unseen factor. A famous example is the number of Nicholas Cage movies and pool drownings in the US, which are mathematically linked but purely coincidental. Another case is the correlation of ice cream sales and shark attacks, which is triggered by the hidden variable of warm weather. The latter promotes ice cream purchases and encourages swimming, which enables shark attacks. More examples can be found online.[9]

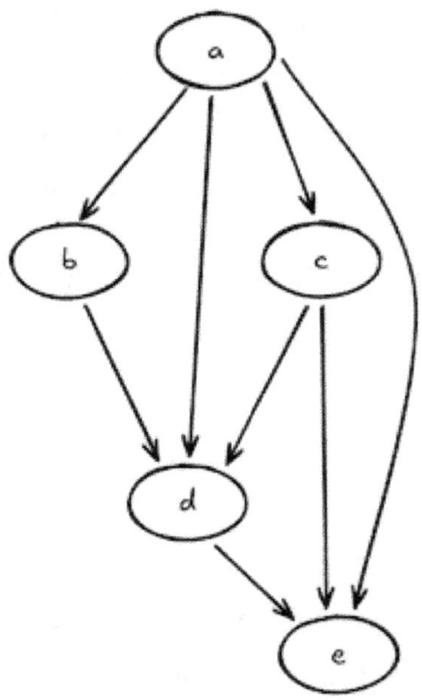

Figure 7: Example of a directed acyclic graph.

Again, we can treat this as a small data project and follow our trusted processes. The important steps this time are surfacing assumptions and, if applicable, experimenting. To document the assumptions about the connection, we can use a directed acyclic graph (DAG). This is, if we oversimplify, a drawing depicting the various influences (or connections) between components, called vertices, within the concept of a DAG. To the side, we see a neutral example of such a graph: "a" leads to "c,"

9https://www.tylervigen.com/spurious-correlations

which in turn leads to "e." We will create the same lineage for our two variables and their possible alternative influences. The valuable part is every connection, called an edge, that is not a direct link between variable 1 and variable 2. Within that, we might already identify the alternative explanations. This exploration seems similar to the "using different perspectives" step in critical thinking. But here we are starting with it as we examine the results of an analytical process or an observation.

Once alternatives have been explored, we can experiment to validate these new hypotheses. We can run new experiments if the circumstances allow, or we can use already gathered data for verification. In the latter case, the evaluation of the sources must ensure that we do not fall into the trap of confirmation bias. By that, we mean that the data can only confirm what has already been found, either through inherent bias or biased selection. Experiments with existing data can be conducted across different periods or markets to test the same observation. A rule of thumb is that real effects travel while coincidences do not. Another experiment to run is to examine whether variable 1 also moves another outcome/variable, which it should not. If so, we are observing noise.

If the spuriousness has been identified, we need to communicate the possibility of disappointment. The DAG from earlier can be a visual aid. We can include the costs of being wrong, in either way, as an argument for caution.

Requirement fog

Another known trope in data work is the unspecified request or problem. There can be multiple reasons for the fog: ambiguous goals, unspecified success criteria, conflicting stakeholders, shifting terms (as shown above), or hidden constraints.

We have encountered a process that skipped the step of "Framing the Problem." Going back to our general guidelines, we have to start with specifying which decision or change we want to enable, by whom, and by when. A one-liner, as shown in the example in Chapter 1, can be sufficient. Next, we outline the constraints and assumptions by working with all relevant stakeholders. In case of conflicts between their inputs, we can act as a mediator, but we do not need to carry the burden of resolving the issue. Shared glossaries and concrete examples can be supporting tools. Along the way, we can use our understanding of communication to provide a path towards clarity, documenting the steps and final outcome in ways that are understandable and widely accessible.

Dashboard overload

Not only producers of data benefit from critical thinking and communication, but consumers do as well. The most common circumstance is dashboard overload. In a worst-case scenario, it is a sprawl of unowned, duplicative, context-free pages that raise cognitive load and erode trust. And even in the best case, it is an unintelligible collection of information. Considering our communication model from earlier, we realize that the channel capacity has been reached; the message is not lost due to noise but to truncation.

The cause is usually a skipped "Framing the Problem" step again. So we step back and re-evaluate which decision each dashboard enables, for which audience, and on what cadence. Additionally, we assign an owner with the respective decision rights. It is also likely that we will discover some metric drift in this issue, which we will resolve as outlined above. The audit should not just happen at the dashboard level, but also at the level of each chart or table, as each component should serve a distinct purpose. The outcomes of the audit need to be documented and clearly communicated, or distributed respectively. In case this was the first occurrence of such a revision, we can also use it to establish a routine check practice. In general, should this kind of review happen regularly as part of the data product lifecycle, and not only when consumers start to complain, or worse, stop accessing or using the assets provided by data teams?

Critical thinking, communication, and data culture

Most organizations seek to become data-driven, to create a data culture. The promise behind that is that data will provide answers to all questions and, therefore, will drive the success of the enterprise. But there are two challenges to that. Firstly, not all innovations can be derived from data. The iPhone, for instance, was not an answer coming out of a dashboard but a clever combination of existing technologies. Secondly, no one really knows what data culture entails, or whether there is a general definition.

Let us start with the basics. Culture, as defined by anthropologists, consists of symbols, language, norms, rituals, and artifacts:

- **Symbols.** Symbols are physical things or behaviors that stand for something else. A common real-world example that has even transcended into the digital realm is the gesture of a thumbs-up representing approval. By now, this symbol can be found on almost any digital platform as a "like" or general show of support. But there are exceptions. This gesture is considered rude in parts of Africa, Greece, Russia, and elsewhere. The lesson being: the symbols are closely tied to the individual culture and not universal. In the data world, an example of a symbol is a Northstar Key Performance Indicator (KPI), which represents the organization's goals. If it is not, it needs to be reworked. And again, the same KPI, by name or calculation method, can imply different approaches across organizations.

- **Language.** Language refers to a shared vocabulary, definitions, and idioms. The perfect example is the use of English in this book, written in the Roman alphabet. There are rules for how letters must look and how they form words and sentences. The data world knows the value of a shared vocabulary and definitions of metrics and central entities. These provide a foundation for clear, actionable communication with the business, driving the necessary changes. The main challenge of language in a data context is the constant use and required updates, which occur at a higher rate than in normal languages. The best documented vocabulary is meaningless if not in use by everyone.

- **Norms.** Norms describe standards and expectations for behaving. Consider it a societal pressure to adhere to written and unwritten laws. Theft is frowned upon in most societies, as is loudly chewing your food. The former is sanctioned with punishments of varying degrees; the latter is met with just contempt. The data world can employ norms in two ways: either through data governance, which establishes the official rules governing data within the organization, or by fostering a mindset that prioritizes truth-seeking over status-seeking or curiosity over certainty.

- **Rituals.** Rituals are established procedures and ceremonies, anything that is done repeatedly and intentionally. Usually, they serve a distinct purpose but can lose that cause over time. Wearing neckties stems from military uniforms of Croatian mercenaries in the 17th century and has since become a symbol for professionalism. Other examples of rituals include weddings, our morning coffee, and the Olympic Games every four years. In the context of data, we can find rituals such as regular metric reviews, postmortems, or a metric-centric section at every all-hands meeting. The important part is that those do not become meaningless rituals but get iterated upon when necessary.

- **Artifacts.** Artifacts are the (physical) things culture leaves behind. It describes everything made by the individuals of the respective culture, usually for distinct purposes. Everything around us is an artifact: our tools, our clothing, our homes. But music and other forms of artistic expression are also artifacts. Looking back at the data world, we will find metrics and data contracts, glossaries, decision logs, and many other forms of documentation. All the data products, from data lakes to dashboards to fine-tuned machine learning models, are artifacts as well.

So how do those concepts align with critical thinking and communication? Firstly, communication is the only way to transfer or propagate the elements we looked at above. At the same time, many of those elements serve a communicative purpose. Communication creates transparency if we share the truth in its entirety. Transparency creates alignment, as every part of the organization can understand the current state and how its work can support reaching the next goals. This can be supported by clear ownership of data and data products across the company, as well as shared semantics. A glossary manifests the latter.

Critical thinking as part of a data culture, or as a seed for creating one, provides input for the norms and rituals and their underlying values. We could call it organized skepticism in the decision process. And by that, we do not mean challenging everything just for the sake of challenging. As mentioned with rituals, we do not want to lose the intended purpose. Part of this skepticism can be the use of a symbol like "The Other Chair" or "The Empty Shoes," which embody the need for scrutiny and the taking of alternative perspectives before latching onto conclusions.

A central tool for a growing data culture is feedback loops, referring to the reflection part of critical thinking and the need for transparency. Only by listening to stakeholders can the data culture adapt and develop. Data is not a purpose in itself, except for very few specific business cases. Through feedback, we learn what works, what does not, and can adjust in the next cycle or the next data project. The talks themselves are another ritual that spreads the values we want to instill: openness to other perspectives and the understanding that there is often no absolute truth.

Below, we collected some forms in which the principles of critical thinking and communication can shape your data culture.

	Critical Thinking	Communication
Symbols	"The Other Chair"	Key Performance Indicators
Language	Hypotheses, assumptions, risks	Glossary, Naming conventions, Metric inventory
Norms	Evidence over Rank Reversible over perfect	Clarity over Cleverness
Rituals	Decision reviews & Retros Pre-Mortems	Listening over Speaking
Artifacts	Risk Matrix	Data Products Data Contracts

Figure 8: Cultural elements of critical thinking and communication.

Case studies

Here are some examples of how a lack of critical thinking, communication, or both caused issues in the data world.

Google Flu Trends (GFT), a former Google Product, famously overestimated influenza prevalence because search behavior and media attention confounded the signal.[10] The original intention was to

[10] https://pubmed.ncbi.nlm.nih.gov/24626916/

use search requests around common symptoms and related terms to predict flu activity. But there were issues. For one, people researching symptoms do not automatically have the flu. Additionally, media coverage of flu seasons contributed to the skew, as people were still querying about the topics regardless of their own health situation. In 2013, GFT overshot the real-life prevalence by up to 140%. Multiple adjustments were made, but the product was ultimately canceled. The refusal to accept other reasons or perspectives for search behavior led to this outcome. The science post-mortem labeled this "big data hubris" and urged pairing model outputs with traditional surveillance and explicit assumption checks. Clearer communication about scope, limits, and updating rules would have made the correlations safe to act on. Interestingly, simpler approaches like recency heuristics, using the last outbreak as a predictor, outperformed the large model.

The 1999 loss of the Mars Climate Orbiter, a probe intended to observe the weather on our neighboring planet, was traced to a units mismatch.[11] Something we mentioned earlier was metric drift or unaligned semantics. Two teams working on the Orbiter lacked communication. Lockheed Martin software produced thruster data in pound-force seconds, while navigation software at JPL expected newton-seconds. This reveals a basic failure of shared definitions across an interface. This mismatch led to incorrect position data during entry into Mars orbit, resulting in the loss of the probe. What we can learn from this is not to base our communication on assumptions, but rather on fixed contracts or definitions, which are artifacts we mentioned above. Additionally, we need to ensure testing of outcomes and active experimentation before go-live.

Key takeaways

- Data work can fail in many ways outside the actual technical or mathematical workflow, or by applying the methods without questioning them, like ice cream and shark attacks.
- Data science can be approached with the Scientific Method.
- Data culture is a direct result of applied critical thinking and proper communication.

11 https://llis.nasa.gov/llis_lib/pdf/1009464main1_0641-mr.pdf

CHAPTER 3

How Critical Thinking, Communication, and Ethical Action Improve Data Work

"Many people think of data science as a job, but it's more accurate to think of it as a way of thinking, a means of extracting insights through the scientific method."

Thilo Huellmann

We've already looked at the issues of a lack of critical thinking, communication, and ethics in data work, and the drama that ensues from that, but how does this trifecta work in practice to make things better? And most importantly, how does the framework add value to the whole process, challenging yourself and others, to find better solutions?

In this chapter, we'll look at just that, along with how acting responsibly and ethically organically complements this framework. We'll also explore a realistic example of how all three work together to make data more effective and robust. Following that, we'll explore a case study that you can also use as an exercise to make all this material your own.

Critical thinking in practice

Asking the right questions

When Thomas Watson (among others) said, "asking the right question is more than halfway to the right answer," he was on to something. There is power in formulating accurate questions that focus attention on the crux of a matter and guide an investigation towards the aspects of a problem that are most needed. This may be one of the key aspects of critical thinking as it's an enabling force, a superpower of sorts, that makes it possible for us to penetrate the veil of ignorance that makes something a problem. If you have an interest in problem-solving, it may be because of this playful dialogue within you that makes a problem unravel as you dig deeper into its key elements, uncovering potential solutions and evaluating them to find the best one. It all starts with a single question or two, however.

The topic of questions was covered thoroughly in a previous book ("Question-driven Data Projects", 2024). It's important that the data work include both data projects and initiatives, as the right questions can also help clarify the bigger picture. Just like critical thinking isn't only for the details, the right questions are also relevant to all levels of data work.

It's important to note here that not all questions are created equal. This is why this section is titled "asking the **right** questions." What makes a question right, though? Unfortunately, there is no black-and-white answer to this. Suffice to say that a question that takes you into a quest towards the answer you need to tackle a problem or come up with an insight, in an efficient way, is more right than its alternatives. It's crucial not to get caught up in an obsessive optimization process at this point, as it's hard to gauge the validity of a question before it's tested. Critical thinking guards against that, ensuring your questions gradually become more focused and overall "right." Some key questions to ask, or at least use as starting points to formulate your case-specific questions, are the following:

- Why? (To get to the root cause of something)
- How? (To understand how something works)
- What if? (To explore alternative approaches to the same thing)

Beyond these key questions, which are more related to the Analyzing stage of the Bloom Revised Taxonomy (BRT) we talked about in a previous chapter, there are also a few more that are geared towards the Evaluating stage:

- So what? (To understand the importance of something and its consequences)
- What's next? (To figure out what stems from this course of action)
- How should this be prioritized? (To put something into perspective)

Note that, just as the mother sauces of food science are fundamental in developing other sauces relevant to a particular dish, these questions can be viewed as the building blocks for your customized questions, tailored to your data-related endeavors.

Validating data and insights

Validating data and insights is a natural next step to all this, and it's closely linked to the evaluating stage of the BRT. This helps filter out all the redundant or noisy information from the mix, allowing us to focus on the most promising data and insights. In the context of questions, this validation process is about identifying which questions are most relevant and which answers are worth exploring further. This way, we can conserve our attention and resources in general, making the most of them for tackling the problems at hand.

Validating data ensures the data is clean, relevant, and unbiased. The process involves cleaning and organizing the data (removing noise, normalizing values, and properly coding variables), then verifying its relevance to the project's goals, often a prediction task. Using statistical metrics, heuristics, and algorithms, we assess relationships between variables and identify biases. Balancing the dataset, whether by collecting or generating new data, helps mitigate these biases. This iterative process is time-consuming and complex, especially with multiple data streams, but it yields a functional, balanced dataset.

Validating insights means evaluating their relevance and value to the project. While insights may seem interesting, the key questions are: Do they address the original objectives? How do they align with the data strategy? Which insights should be prioritized or explored further? Filtering insights this way ensures they contribute meaningfully. Reflecting on lessons learned, beyond the insights themselves, helps refine the project's direction and deepen understanding of the challenges ahead.

Validating is crucial to critical thinking, as it puts everything into perspective and helps us reflect more deeply on what we have.

Failing to apply this crucial step may lead to or contribute to an array of issues, such as the cognitive traps we'll discuss in the next subsection.

Avoiding cognitive traps

Cognitive traps and similar pitfalls are often unavoidable, at least when we start, but they are just there to test us and refine our thinking. If we view them this way, they can be stepping stones towards a better way of thinking and a valuable experience overall.

A typical cognitive trap is that of perfectionism. This involves trying to get everything right, from the questions to the validation, and every syllogism in between. However, this isn't realistic and may trap you in an over-optimization loop that never ends. The funny thing is that even if you were to get this process perfect, it would be of no use since it's bound to change as new data becomes available. The refined questions you came up with may no longer be applicable, and you'll need to develop new validations and connections for all the new information that becomes available. To avoid this trap, it's best to set a limited time to do all your critical thinking for a data project and stick to it. The law of diminishing returns will see to it that additional time won't make that much of a difference anyway, something that you are better off realizing sooner rather than later.

Excessive exploration is another common cognitive trap. This has to do with getting lost in the questioning part of the process and in the endless possibilities. Instead of validating and taking action, you may end up contemplating endlessly the various questions that present themselves and the possible answers that stem from them. This is similar to the perfectionism trap, though more focused on the questions stage. However, this doesn't lead anywhere, and it's akin to exploring the different variants of a chess opening without ever trying them out in a real game. It's best to explore additional questions, if time allows, once the first iteration of the data project is completed. At that point, the questions are also bound to be more interesting and yield better results.

A final commonly encountered cognitive trap is losing track of your thought process and letting it go aimlessly. This concerns completing the critical thinking process repeatedly, but without making any real progress on your data-related objectives. In other words, you analyze data for the sake of it, getting more and more out of context. It's one thing coming up with new methods and metrics for data analysis, also known as research and development work, and it's a completely different story if you continue with a data project without answering any of the original questions satisfactorily.

Having a plan of thought

To put all of this into perspective and be able to communicate it effectively to others, we need a plan that maps our thoughts and connects them meaningfully. There are business-related questions that need to be addressed, and all the data work we undertake (in whatever capacity suits our roles) must be aligned with them.

The purpose of a data strategy is to inspire a plan of thought that guides our critical thinking more effectively.

The plan of thought is important, particularly when you are ready to externalize your thoughts to others, enabling fruitful communication. Having the end result in mind before embarking on a critical thought journey can help you stay accountable and focused, making the most of this process.

Communication in practice

Tailoring the message

Knowing your audience is one of the most fundamental aspects of communication and a great starting point. You wouldn't deliver the same speech to a group of techies as you would to a group of non-technical people, for example. While technical jargon can be useful, it may deter some individuals and make communication more challenging. Also, even if they are aware of the terms as buzzwords, they may not comprehend the nuances involved, and this disparity is bound to derail the communication sooner or later. A good way around this issue is to observe other people's vocabulary and try to use similar words as much as possible. If they use a technical term, make sure they know what it means before you include it in conversation. Sometimes, explaining it and giving examples that your audience can relate to can go a long way.

Having different layers in your message or your insights report can also be a big plus. This way, you can make sure that everyone gets something from it, while the additional layers may encourage people to dig deeper into what you say or write. The multiple layers can also spark a sense of wonder, which is the best thing you can achieve in a communication, as it can engage your audience more and make them more interested in the data, the processes you followed, and the insights. Things may appear simple at a high level, but some nuances need to be explored, and it's your role to make them accessible and interesting. There is a reason why most people care more about a story than a list of facts, even if the latter has its place.

Keeping the insights relevant to the areas of interest of the stakeholders is also paramount. This is another way to keep your audience engaged and your insights applicable. You may come up with an interesting finding like "customers of cohort A tend to buy product B during the weekends," but how is this useful to your stakeholders? Perhaps tell them that leveraging this insight can help drive sales of product B by 15% (or whatever the proportion of cohort A is during the weekend), and you may get more traction. Also, if you drop suggestions like starting a marketing campaign for product B targeting the people in cohort A, this may make the insight more relevant. Regardless, the insights have value, but "selling" them to stakeholders requires effort beyond traditional data work, making tailoring the message part of the communication crucial.

Storytelling with data

Telling a story is one of the best ways to keep your audience engaged and retain the whole message in memory. Storytelling isn't easy, however, as it involves creativity and a different kind of communication, in which you view the whole message from the other person's point of view. Also, the fewer things you assume they know beforehand, the better. The good news is that the more you practice with this, the easier storytelling will become for you over time. The key is to have a strong core (the story's message) and make it accessible in different ways.

Storytelling is even more powerful with the right props, such as graphics and animations. Much like a good word processing software would make it easy for you to pick a font by showing you samples of the available fonts in the corresponding drop-down box, a good data-driven story would be easier to follow if there are props that anchor the audience's attention. These don't need to be fancy plots; they just need to be meaningful and self-explanatory. The graphics need to be so self-contained that, even out of context, someone can still understand what they say. Animations are the same as graphics that involve movement. Both graphics and animations can add a lot to a story.

Storytelling is also about having a good understanding of the work behind the insights and conveying that in your presentation. In other words, for a story to be delivered well, it's always a good idea to have some skin in the game of the project behind it. That's why AI-generated videos, although elegant, may not carry the same weight when delivering a story. The storytelling process is also often interactive, with people asking questions, making comments, and adding observations. This is part of the essence of communication, which distinguishes it from a well-crafted monologue. One of the purposes of storytelling is to engage and create a locus of attention through which a deeper discussion of the insights can ensue.

Handling pushback

Naturally, not everyone will agree with your message or the next steps you may suggest. That's why it's important to handle any pushback diplomatically and effectively. Sometimes the pushback has merit in the sense that there is something off with the data project or the insights, and someone points it out to you. Other times, the pushback stems from a misunderstanding, most likely related to the storytelling aspect. After all, it's a learning experience and an opportunity to refine your communication skills. In the scientific community, pushback is not just inevitable but also encouraged as it generates more robust theories and applications. If something isn't challenged enough, especially in the data world, it may become feeble and unreliable. In this chapter's case study, we'll look at clear examples of this happening.

Handling pushback doesn't mean that you need to accept other views without resistance. In fact, if you have faith in your work, you'd want to defend it as much as possible. Also, if the pushback has merit, you may adopt the parts that make sense for the project and refine your process accordingly. It's not a black-or-white situation, and there is often room for creative adjustments, especially for complex datasets and sophisticated models. It could be, for example, that the data model you used wasn't the best, but the features you developed were fine, so all you need to do is choose another data model. Also, it might be that the evaluation metric you used wasn't the best, and you just need to redo some steps while leveraging a different one. Be flexible.

Handling pushback is essential for refining the data project and improving its value-adds. This is a more psychological skill that involves detachment, a beginner's mind, and a holistic perspective. The project is bigger than any one of its contributors, and it takes a special kind of courage to acknowledge and apply this fact. Doing so enables you to detach from it and act in a way that benefits the project, even if it feels like you are losing ground personally. This, however, is essential for a proper handling of pushback as it enables you to make refinements to the project by using the energy of the pushback to your advantage. This translates to better value-adds for the project, as it leverages more information (beyond the data it is based on). Handling pushback is a powerful skill that can, at the very least, greatly improve your communication skills.

Learning from feedback

Feedback can be very educational on many levels. Whether it's the data analysis part of the project, the insights derived, or the communication of it all, it's still useful because it enables you to refine your process and improve over time. The feedback is not necessarily personal but rather relates to the particular project and the delivery of the findings. As such, you can distance yourself from it and view it as yet another data point, one that relates to your craft, too. Learning from feedback also helps build rapport with your audience and be a better team player.

Feedback is a powerful tool for improving data processes and projects in many ways. This is particularly the case when the feedback comes from a genuine interest in improving the project and those involved in it (i.e., true mentoring and leadership). This can shed light on your blind spots and raise awareness of aspects of the projects that were done mechanically or without sufficient depth. This makes feedback probably the best educational tool for data professionals at all levels, something that can benefit the corresponding data initiative too in various ways.

Despite our sophisticated frameworks and computer systems, we don't know everything about every dataset, and with the feedback aspect of communication, we become aware of this and improve ourselves and our work.

Acting responsibly/ethically

Identifying and mitigating bias

Biases are everywhere these days, and given a large enough dataset, you are bound to find them there, too. Things could be worse, though; you could fail to find the biases altogether (while they are still there). With modern datasets being so vast and complex, it's unlikely that you'll find all the biases present, but finding the most striking ones is often good enough. Of course, the impact of the biases often depends on how much they are exposed to the end user. In modern AI systems where biases can find their way into the model's outputs, the problem is often more pronounced, triggering some users. So, the responsible thing would be to tackle them preemptively and, if you fail to do so, be open to user feedback so you can identify the remaining biases and address them in the next iteration of the system.

Measuring bias in a variable is relatively easy. However, as the dataset becomes more complex, with more variables, biases become a greater nuisance. This is especially the case when text data is involved, where biases are more subtle and span many different verticals. So, as a first step, you can decide on what biases to focus on and how to measure them. Then, you can start measuring those biases in your datasets or the outputs of your AI models. Perhaps you can even automate at least part of this whole process, making it more scalable. Measuring bias is best done with specialized heuristics developed for this purpose and, when available, taking into consideration users' feedback. Keeping a human in the loop can also be useful, as biases can sometimes be very subtle and elude the metrics used.

Mitigating bias is more challenging, especially in datasets with more variables or text. This involves actively changing the dataset by removing excessive rows, adding new ones, or a combination of both. In cases where complex text-based datasets are involved, additional data streams may be the best strategy (to complement the existing ones). This bias mitigation process needs to be accompanied by periodic bias measurement to ensure progress and that we don't fall into the other extreme (bias). It's not an easy process, but given enough data and intelligent changes to the dataset, it's feasible. However, it can be quite time-consuming, so it's best to plan it properly. Having an overall bias metric that covers different bias verticals would make the process more manageable and faster.

Transparency and accountability

Transparency is key for ethical and responsible data work, and therefore, should be used in most sophisticated data models, particularly AI-related ones. In fact, there are laws in the EU on that (namely, the EU AI Act we talked about in Chapter 2). So, having this quality in an organization is not just about ethics. How can we expect our data systems to be transparent if we can't be transparent ourselves? Transparency also fosters better rapport in a team and makes collaboration much easier. However, it's not easy, as it's often easier to let things be covered by a veil of mystery, especially if there are bugs or data-related issues present and those responsible want to keep them secret. This brings us to the other part of ethics that goes hand in hand with transparency: accountability.

Accountability is about taking ownership of the processes you undertake in a data project. This leads to more responsible data professionals and better communication among data team members and with other stakeholders. Good communication, especially between the team leader and the other team members, can foster a sense of accountability among everyone. When you are connected with the rest of the team and understand its pains and aspirations, it's much easier to take part in it and act more responsibly. Accountability is something we all have, and it stems naturally from a good sense of critical thinking.

Transparency and accountability are essential for ethical data work for other reasons, too. For example, they can foster a culture of trust and meritocracy in the organization. This not only can further nourish critical thinking and communication, but can also make data initiatives easier through better collaboration. Transparency and accountability are key aspects of ethics and are very practical. It's no coincidence that they are often valued more than other skills in the workplace and remain relevant even amid the various disruptions new technologies like AI bring. Besides, it's unlikely they will ever become obsolete or less important, especially as technology makes people more capable in the so-called hard skills. This latter fact makes softer skills even more important, and what better way to foster them than by expressing character traits like transparency and accountability in your day-to-day work?

Advocating for ethical practices

Ethical practices are like monetary tokens; the more people have them, the more useful they are. However, just as ideas do, they require effort to propagate and become known to people. That's why advocating for ethical practices is so important. Much like critical thinking and communication, ethical practices improve our lives and make our data projects more efficient. Yet, without actively promoting them, it's doubtful that they will reach enough people on their own to show their value at a noticeable level. Naturally, they are better off being promoted through positions of leadership, as this can enable them to have a larger reach.

However, advocating for ethical practices is something everyone can do in some capacity. You don't need to be an ethicist to know what's right in your line of work and talk about it to others in your field or adjacent fields. Acting on that knowledge is the most important way to promote it. Naturally, having skills in critical thinking and communication can complement that significantly, making the whole process more effective. Additionally, each of these three skills helps the others, as they constitute a framework of sorts for being a better professional. This is especially the case for data work, where ethical matters are abundant and require us to act accordingly. Through all this, we can lead by example and be the best that we can be in our roles, inspiring others around us to do the same.

Promoting ethical practices isn't a one-time thing, though. To be effective, this needs to be done constantly or at least periodically. Although the best way to do this is by example, sometimes additional strategies, such as seminars, workshops, and other forms of professional training, can also be valuable. Additionally, rewarding ethical behavior within a team or the organization can be beneficial. This doesn't need to happen in a flashy way, but recognizing ethical action organically can go a long way. The important thing is to eventually make ethical practices part of the organization's culture and foster them in everyone, regardless of their role. This can help with critical thinking, communication, and other aspects of day-to-day life.

Interconnection of critical thinking, communication, and ethics

Let's now look at an example of how critical thinking, communication, and ethics work together in a real-world situation. Namely, let's explore how the fictitious company GreenCart, which provides an e-commerce grocery delivery service, plans to put together a data-driven loyalty program to reward its high-value customers and reduce churn overall.

As a first step, we can define the problem at hand, something that's clearly a critical thinking process. It involves questioning assumptions and figuring out what exactly we need to do. Potential questions to ask are:

- What does "high-value customer" actually mean? Is it just about how much they spend, or also about frequency, referrals, or engagement with our site?
- Could the definition we use exclude certain groups (for instance, lower-income customers who are also loyal)?

When it comes to validation, we can analyze available data to identify correlations between customer behavior and churn. We can also spot biases, such as the model favoring high-spending urban customers and overlooking rural ones, who, although less frequent, are long-term customers. We can also reflect on our findings and consider next steps.

As a second step, we build and validate the model, something that involves both critical thinking and ethics. During this step, the team builds a predictive model to identify customers for the loyalty program and also validates it for fairness. This is crucial as the latter part isn't always included in the model development process, especially when the deadlines are tight.

The ethical check involved may be something like:

- Does this model disadvantage any group (for instance, a demographic or geographic group)?
- How fair is this model for the end-user overall?

In this scenario, the model is found to underweight rural customers as it prioritizes order frequency over other factors, such as customer longevity. To remedy this, we retrain the model to take customer tenure and referral activity into account, rather than just how much they spend. To test the new model's fairness, we can run it and check whether any group is systematically excluded from the high-value customer classification.

In the critical thinking aspect of this step, counterfactual analysis (*what-if* questions) is employed, along with fairness analysis for the ethics part.

The third step of this scenario involves communicating findings with the stakeholders. This involves presenting the model, along with its limitations, to marketing and leadership. For this to be effective, we need to tailor the message to the different audiences.

For example, when talking to executives, we can focus on ROI and risk mitigation by stating, "This new approach will reduce churn by 14% while avoiding any bias-related PR risks." When talking to the marketing team, we can emphasize the customer segments involved and the corresponding messaging by stating, for example, "Rural customers respond better to referral rewards than discounts." Visuals would be required to drive home the points we make in these communications. For example, before-and-after charts depicting how the adjusted model now includes more diverse customers, as well as graphics showing this increase in diversity.

As for the storytelling aspect of the communication, this can be done by framing the initiative as "a fairer way to reward loyalty," or something along those lines, highlighting the ethical aspects of this approach. From that, we can weave a narrative that's relatable and understandable, with minimal technical jargon.

The fourth step is all about implementation and monitoring, which involves both critical thinking and ethics. This step entails launching the program and monitoring for unintended consequences and model drift.

When it comes to ethics, it is all about transparency and feedback. Namely, we need to clearly communicate to customers how the new initiative works (i.e., rewards based on both tenure and money spent). As for feedback, we need to set up a system for customers to express concerns and report perceived unfairness.

Regarding critical thinking, we can conduct checks such as A/B tests and bias monitoring. A/B tests can compare churn rates before and after the new model is deployed to determine whether there is a significant improvement. The bias monitoring can track whether any groups are still under-represented in rewards and, if so, by how much.

As ethics is crucial here, we can also include impact assessment and customer surveys. Namely, we can conduct periodic reviews of the program's fairness (e.g., every quarter) and surveys focused on specific aspects of fairness.

Finally, as a fifth step, we look into iterating and improving the model. This involves using feedback to continuously refine the program, applying critical thinking, communication, and ethics in tandem.

When it comes to critical thinking and ethics, we can use them to discover that older customers were churning because they preferred phone orders (something the model couldn't track). To leverage this information, we can add phone-order data to the model and expand rewards for older customers who prefer phone ordering.

When it comes to communication, we can present updates to stakeholders, such as "we have improved the program to include X group. Here's the relevant data and the ethical rationale." Naturally, we'd use some graphics for this communication too.

In this step, we can see interconnection in action more than anywhere else in this scenario. First, critical thinking spots a gap in a process (older customers); then ethics ensures the fix is fair to the people involved; and finally, communication gets buy-in for all changes deemed necessary. You can view a visual of this example's workflow in Figure 9.

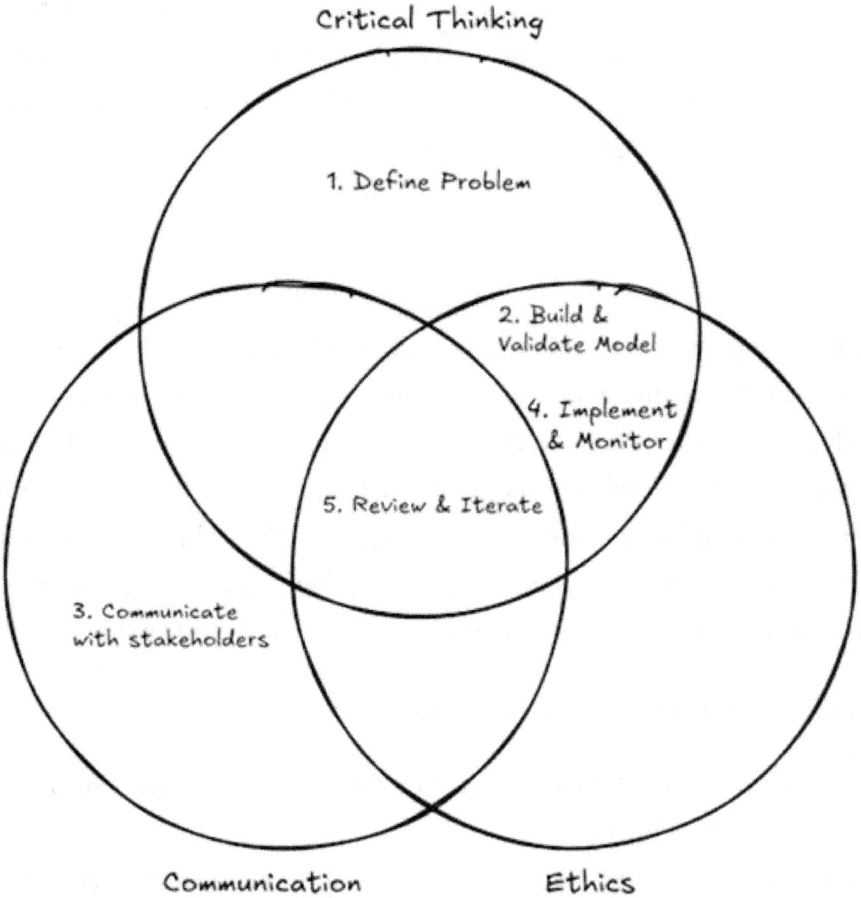

Figure 9: Interconnectivity between critical thinking, communication, and ethics in a realistic example.

Case study: The flawed churn prediction model

Naturally, not all scenarios are so well-planned and executed. However, with proper critical thinking and communication, even a problematic situation can be alleviated. In this case, let's look at an imaginary company called *StreamFlix*, which is a mid-sized streaming service with five million subscribers.

The problem is that customer churn was rising, and the data team was tasked with building a predictive model to identify at-risk subscribers and reduce cancellations by preventing them whenever possible. The data team then built a model using historical data (watch time, payment history, customer support interactions, etc.) and deployed it to flag "high-risk" users for targeted retention campaigns (discounts, personalized recommendations, etc.). So far, so good. However, things didn't go exactly as expected...

What went wrong?

In this scenario, there were several failures across all three verticals and their interconnectivity. In the realm of critical thinking, there was the issue of unquestioned assumptions. The team assumed their historical data was representative of all users. However, the dataset was biased. It over-represented older, wealthier subscribers (who had been with the company longer) and underrepresented younger, lower-income users (who churned faster but were a growing segment). The model ignored geographic and cultural factors (for instance, users in regions with poor internet infrastructure were flagged as "high-risk" simply because they streamed less).

There were also a few red flags that were missed altogether:

- No one asked things like "Does this dataset reflect our current user base, or just our longest-standing customers?"
- The team didn't validate the model's predictions against real-world user feedback.

As far as communication is concerned, there was the issue of misaligned messaging. The data team presented the model's findings to marketing as a list of "high-risk users" without explaining:

- Why certain users were flagged (for instance, "low watch time" could mean poor internet, not disinterest).
- Limitations of the model (for instance, "This doesn't account for new user segments").

Marketing acted on the data blindly, sending discounts to wealthier users (who didn't need them) and ignoring younger users (who were actually at higher risk of churning).

The result was a campaign that failed to reduce churn and wasted $200K on discounts for the wrong users.

The ethical failure was also noteworthy, and it involved unintended consequences. The model disproportionately flagged users from lower-income regions as "high-risk" due to their streaming habits, leading to:

- Fewer retention efforts for these users (since they were mislabeled).
- Reinforcement of bias: The model's predictions became a self-fulfilling prophecy, as neglected users churned even faster.

No one considered the ethical implications of the model's recommendations or audited it for fairness.

How critical thinking, communication, and ethics saved the day

After the failed campaign, the team revisited the problem with a focus on critical thinking, communication, and ethics. Regarding critical thinking, they took action as follows:

Asked relevant questions, such as:

- "What groups might our dataset exclude or misrepresent?"
- "How might our model's predictions harm certain users?"

Validated the model:

- Conducted a bias audit and found the model was 3x more likely to misclassify users from lower-income regions.
- Expanded the dataset to include newer, more diverse users.
- Reflected on the whole problem:
    - Pondered on the problem anew and better understood its nuances.
    - Documented all relevant findings for future reference.

As far as communication was concerned, they resolved to do the following:

Improved delivery through storytelling:

- Presented findings to marketing as a story: "Our model was like a doctor diagnosing patients without checking their medical history. Here's how we fixed it!"

- Adapted the story to different audiences, ensuring that everyone could relate to it.

Used visuals to show:

- Which user segments were misclassified and why?
- How the new model would prioritize younger, at-risk users.

Clarified limitations:

- Explained that the model was one tool among many and should be combined with user surveys and support feedback.

As for ethics, they acted in a way that enabled the rebuilding of trust with the customers:

Redesigned the model:

- Added fairness constraints to reduce bias (e.g., using equal weights across regions).
- Monitored predictions for disparate impact on different user groups.

Transparency with users:

- Sent a clear, empathetic email to previously neglected users: "We realized our system wasn't serving you fairly. Here's how we're fixing it and a discount to thank you for sticking with us."

Final result:

- Churn dropped by 20% in the targeted segments.
- The company rebuilt trust with underrepresented users.

Key lessons

By thinking critically about this case study, we can derive the following insights that can be applied in various other situations and data projects:

Critical thinking:

- Always ask, "What assumptions am I making? Who might be excluded or harmed by this data?"
- Validate models with real-world feedback, not just historical data.

Communication:

- Translate technical findings into stories and visuals for non-technical stakeholders.
- Be transparent about limitations: don't let data speak for itself.

Ethics:

- Audit models for bias before and after deployment.
- Act on ethical red flags: don't wait for a crisis to fix fairness issues.

Critical thinking, communication, and ethics reinforce each other. Skipping one (for instance, ethics) can undermine the others (for instance, trust in your data), especially in the long run. Working together, these elements of thought and action enable a more proactive approach that's easier for others to work towards, improving them in the process.

Key takeaways

- Formulating precise, purpose-driven questions (for instance, *Why? How? What if? So what?*) is foundational to critical thinking (especially in data work) as it clarifies problems, guides analysis, and avoids wasted effort. Questions evolve with experience and should balance depth with practicality.

- Validating data (cleanliness, relevance, bias) and insights (alignment with goals) is essential, but over-optimization (perfectionism, excessive exploration, or aimless analysis) derails progress.

- A structured *plan of thought*, tied to business objectives, keeps efforts focused and actionable.

- Adapt language to audience; layer insights for depth; link findings to stakeholder interests with actionable suggestions.
- Frame insights as a narrative, use clear, self-explanatory visuals, and invite interaction to deepen engagement.
- Stay open to critique; defend valid work but refine where needed; use feedback to strengthen the project.
- Treat feedback as data to improve analysis, communication, and teamwork; detach ego for growth.
- Proactively identify high-impact biases in data/AI outputs; measure them using heuristics and user feedback; mitigate them via dataset adjustments (removal/addition) or complementary data streams. Iterate periodically.
- Document processes openly (especially for AI systems, for instance, EU AI Act compliance); foster team trust and collaboration by addressing issues directly.
- Own decisions and outcomes; encourage open communication to build team responsibility and critical thinking.
- Critical thinking, communication, and ethics work well in tandem when tackling real-world data-related problems. Failure to leverage them can lead to unintended consequences and problems.

CHAPTER 4

Critical Thinking Framework

"Most human beings have an almost infinite capacity for taking things for granted."

Aldous Huxley

Critical thinking is about questioning what we take for granted and making decisions based on the evidence we have (rather than preconceived notions and biases). In data work, taking things for granted would be catastrophic, especially when people's lives or livelihoods are at stake. Equally counter-productive would be to view the available frameworks of critical thinking and accept them as they are. Most of them are fairly recent and were developed with people in mind. What about today's world, where computers are integrated into our decision-making and other aspects of our cognitive processes? If one were to view this matter superficially, they'd inevitably jump to the conclusion that machines can think critically, so we might as well outsource all our cognitive work to the latest and greatest AI assistant. Can you see where we are going with this?

Critical thinking is hard to limit to a framework, and any framework out there is bound to come with its limitations and an expiration date. However, the value of a framework is in how you apply it. Think of it like a plan in a chess game. It may not be the best possible plan (especially when playing with time constraints), but it will have to do. The alternative (playing reactively and thinking little ahead) would most definitely lead to a sub-optimal outcome. Critical thinking frameworks are like that. They are like rough maps that help us navigate the territory of cognitive work, making the most of our assets (business needs, data, and models). If a critical thinking framework can help us improve our decisions, even a little, it can be considered successful. Naturally, if we were to go deeper into it and adapt it to our requirements, the efficiency would improve further.

The critical thinking framework we'll explore in this chapter is based on Dr. Steve Pearlman's work (founder of the *Critical Thinking Institute*), which takes the ideas we introduced in Chapter 1 a step further. This framework is an evolution of the proposed model he uses to teach critical thinking. However, we also borrow elements from Intel's course, *Thinking Critically with Data* (based on Arthur Costa's book, *Developing Minds*), and the *Revised Bloom's Taxonomy* we talked about earlier. We purposefully avoid models like Marzano's taxonomy, which seems like a creative rehash of Bloom's model, with limited emphasis on skepticism or critical inquiry. Nevertheless, we encourage you to explore all critical thinking frameworks you encounter and evaluate them carefully. Perhaps the model that works best for you goes beyond what we cover in this chapter.

To better understand critical thinking, it helps to break it down into a set of main and supplementary cognitive abilities that work together like the different parts of an AI engine. Note that when developing critical thinking, we need all of these, ideally in balance, to make the most of their synergy. Based on our research on the topic, these abilities appear in the table on the facing page.

This list is by no means comprehensive, as you can always dig deeper into these abilities and break them down further. Also, if you were to engage in R&D, you may want to incorporate more creativity-related abilities there, too, since they would be more relevant to this kind of work. The same applies if you were to go into a more specialized kind of critical thinking, such as that related to the management of large groups or entrepreneurship. The key thing to remember is that these are guidelines that aim to inspire a deeper investigation into critical thinking and to provide a rough map for cultivating these abilities in yourself and your team.

Ability	Description	Type
Information gathering	Observing the situation at hand Formulating relevant questions Asking those questions to the right people	
Clarification	Focusing on the most relevant pieces of information and questions Analyzing arguments Engaging in conversation to go deeper on specific questions Applying the Socratic method	Main
Analysis	Breaking down more complex pieces of information Finding relationships among different parts Finding patterns and exploring how they apply to the situation Organizing information into meaningful structures	
Decision making / Evaluation	Judging the credibility of a source Making and judging observations Developing insights for the situation using analyzed information	
Inference / Deep thought	Induction and deduction Judging the validity of deductions and induced arguments Making and evaluating value judgments Making and evaluating suppositional thinking Integrating all critical thinking skills (metacognition)	Main
Methodical thinking	Following problem-solving steps Strategizing Applying metacognition	
Sensitivity to others	Acknowledging others' feelings, level of knowledge, and sophistication Choosing proper forms of communication based on that	
Right rhetorical strategies	Understanding reasoning fallacy terminology Ensuring the avoidance of such fallacies in reasoning and conversation	Suppl.
Applied skepticism	Challenging one's own assumptions, processes, and conclusions Embracing constructive criticism both as a receiver and a giver Encouraging intellectual humility	

To make this whole endeavor more feasible, the following page contains some key skills you may want to focus on, both in educating and in evaluating critical thinkers.

Critical Thinking Skill	Relevant Thinking Processes
Questioning	Problem-posing Hypotheses formulation Critiquing assumptions Exploring alternatives Socratic questioning
Interpreting	Drawing direct inferences Identifying bias Uncovering implicit meanings Contextualizing information Synthesizing perspectives
Qualifying	Recognizing units of basic identity Defining relevant concepts Gathering facts and information in general Recognizing tasks and problems Limiting or specifying scope
Classifying	Recognizing similarities and differences Grouping and sorting information Comparing pieces of info to each other Making either/or distinctions (discerning)
Finding Relationships	Relating parts to each other and with the whole Identifying patterns in information Analyzing information Synthesizing new information Recognizing sequences and order
Transforming	Making analogies Creating metaphors Making initial deductions Coming up with new examples
Drawing Conclusions	Identifying cause and effect Making distinctions High-level Inferring Evaluating information Organizing information
Summarizing	Finding key points Expressing key ideas succinctly Creating mind maps and other diagrams Deeper understanding

Please note that all of this is for educational purposes only. When you apply critical thinking, you don't view it as a series of silos. Instead, there is a structured process, a framework of sorts, that you apply to the problem at hand, adapting it to your circumstances. This consolidates all of the above knowledge; it's easier to remember and can be compiled into know-how that you can make part of your mental process.

The rest of the chapter is organized as follows. First, we'll look into the proposed critical thinking framework that encapsulates all the above ideas into something you can hang in your workspace or screenshot for a presentation. There we'll also look into the nuances of the different stages of critical thinking, particularly their relationships. Following that, we'll look into how critical thinking relates to data work in particular. From pilot projects to more elaborate initiatives, we'll examine the role of this way of thinking and how it can improve the overall workflow. Next, we'll look at a couple of strategies for leveling up your critical thinking and ideas on how you can help your team members do the same. We'll conclude this chapter with a case study of critical thinking in practice and some prompts for you to think about, like an exercise of sorts, to make this more applicable to your situation.

The five stages of critical thinking and how they connect: A more modern approach

It's tempting to think of critical thinking as a linear process comprising the aforementioned abilities and skills. However, just as anything that matters, critical thinking is living and evolving, flexible and adaptable to the situation at hand. In other words, it's something that needs to be experienced and integrated with your mental process. To accomplish that, we need to make it a solid habit.

A first step is to understand it. This is where this framework comes into play. This is an evolution of the work of Dr. Steve Pearlman of the Critical Thinking Institute, with the addition of another, fairly critical aspect, that embodies the concept of metacognition we touched upon earlier. Figure 10 summarizes this whole framework, demonstrating its non-linear functionality. For now, focus on the main stages in bold. We'll get to the bullet points later, as they involve the framework's application to data work.

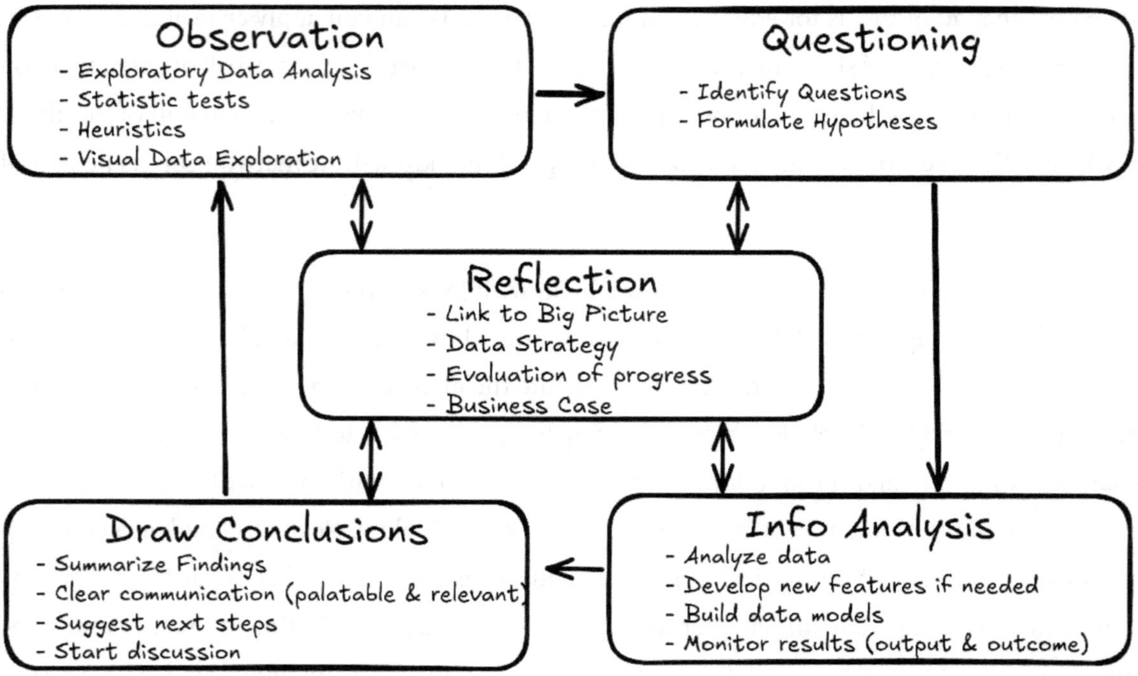

Figure 10: The proposed critical thinking framework for data work, inspired by Dr. Pearlman's work on this subject. All bullet points are merely guidelines of their applicability.

Naturally, it's not as simple as it may first seem. We could write a whole chapter for each one of its stages and probably another one for its relationships. We will explore it in just enough detail so you can practice.

Exploration of each one of the stages

According to this framework, critical thinking comprises observation, questioning, information analysis, and conclusion, with pauses for reflection when needed (ideally after each stage). Even if the bulk of the challenges lie in one or two stages, all stages are important, and we cannot skip any without jeopardizing the overall process's efficacy.

Observation is the most fundamental part of the process,
as it's your interface with the problem at hand.

This can be something external or internal. Observation enables you to gather the necessary facts, explore what's missing, understand what you are after, and gather any relevant information that can bring meaning to all of that. In other words, it's both the key points of the problem and the context. It's important not to underestimate the latter, as it contains all the additional information needed. Naturally, you can't gather everything with just observing, but this stage of critical thinking enables you to have a foundation upon which you can build something solid and useful. Every successful detective (for instance, Sherlock Holmes) often stands out because of their acute observation skills. Chris Thomas, the character introduced in Chapter 1, is no different, even if he's in a different field.

Questioning is an art form and something that distinguishes a good journalist or mentor from a mediocre one. No matter how knowledgeable we are, we don't know everything. Questioning enables you to address knowledge gaps and connect more effectively with the situation you are facing, particularly the people involved.

Speaking of information, information analysis is the most well-known aspect of critical thinking and one that feels closer to home for most people in our field. This involves dissecting the various facts we've gathered, comparing them with what we know and with each other, ensuring there are no logical fallacies, and organizing everything so everyone else can understand it. This can be challenging at times, but even if it's not perfect, it can still be useful. Finding relationships among the different pieces of information is paramount, however, as we need to make the end result something coherent. Think of the entire information set as different arbitrary clusters of points that we need to clean up, clarify, and, most importantly, connect to other clusters, much like a fully connected graph. Even when everything is in black and white, this is a challenging task, let alone when there is ambiguity and uncertainty in the information involved.

Concluding is everyone's favorite activity. However, in the context of critical thinking, it's more of a challenging process than a shortcut to thinking. This involves synthesizing new information (for instance, summaries of the analyzed information), gaining a deeper understanding of the situation at hand, and developing new ideas and action items. It's about making decisions about the information and preparing to act. In this stage of critical thinking, we create something fairly new or, at least, present the information at hand in a novel way that helps us delve deeper into it. It's all about insights and aha moments. Naturally, concluding also ties closely to communication, as it's usually a necessary next step in all our critical thinking endeavors. We'll talk more about that in Chapter 6.

Reflection is a key aspect of critical thinking that's often been ignored, possibly because it's less visible or impressive. Yet its silent profile doesn't mean there isn't a lot of activity there. Reflection enables the intelligent processing of information and the detachment necessary when dealing with a problem. Reflection isn't passive in any way, though. It's mental activity on a different level, like a dialogue without words, a collaborative effort between our analytical and imaginative mental faculties. Reflection is more than just another gear on our mental vehicle, however. It's the ability to make lateral moves or even reverse briefly to get a better perspective of the problem we are tackling. It's unfathomable to have any kind of advanced cognitive process without reflection. That's why it's at the center of the framework and of our thinking in general.

Relationships between stages

You don't need to be an adept critical thinker to deduce that the stages mentioned previously aren't silos. Much like any other applicable knowledge, critical thinking is a dynamic collaboration of components, namely observation, questioning, information analysis, drawing conclusions, and reflection. They are like the five parts of a table (the four legs and the board on top that binds them together); omit one and the whole thing falls apart! Let's dig deeper into this.

First of all, a successful observation stage inevitably leads to better questioning. In fact, these two may even happen simultaneously if you are already familiar with the situation at hand. The different stages of the framework are not silos. Naturally, any assumptions made originally are also put under scrutiny at this point.

Additionally, questioning needs to define the scope to enable better information analysis, effectively laying the ground for the latter. That's why it's crucial to have good questions/hypotheses in hand before analyzing the available information. Some of the information may also be irrelevant, so the questioning stage needs to address that before any processing begins.

Naturally, information analysis requires proper observation and a solid set of facts. Otherwise, we risk getting trapped in the same loops that brought about the problem in the first place. Also, the veracity of these facts needs to be asserted at this stage, though some of that work may have been done through proper questioning. Similarly, the information analysis needs to be done properly (and thoroughly, if time allows) before the drawing conclusions stage begins. Otherwise, the conclusions may not be relevant or even valid.

Finally, without reflection, it's easy to lose track of the bigger picture. This is why, ideally, every single stage should include some reflection on the outcomes and the progress made. Reflection brings about insights and clarifications that may not be possible in the questioning stage, for example, but may be needed to ensure the whole critical thinking process is smooth and efficient. It's like an investment to avoid unnecessary (temporal) costs later on, just as looking at a map once in a while helps you complete a hiking trip as planned and avoid getting lost.

Everyday life examples

So far, the critical thinking topic has been a bit abstract. Let's make it more concrete and relatable with everyday examples. A common scenario is troubleshooting a problematic device or a computer/smartphone application. As technology becomes increasingly complex, it's common to require a strategy for addressing issues with its functionality, to the extent that they can be resolved without a technical expert. This troubleshooting scenario also illustrates the *methodical thinking* aspect of critical thinking.

Dealing with a problematic colleague may seem like an HR matter, but sometimes it can be tackled with critical thinking, at least in the short term. Critical thinking can help us (and, hopefully, the other person too) understand why the problem arises and point to potential solutions. Naturally, this effort needs to be accompanied by proper communication as well.

Learning a new skill related to data work may seem like a simple task with all the books and video tutorials out there, but it takes more than just that. The resources can help you gain the knowledge you need and provide a structure for your learning. Beyond that, however, it's all about how you process it and make it your own, clearly a critical thinking task.

Evaluating the veracity of an announcement about AI is another scenario that's all too common these days. The figureheads who make or broadcast this announcement may be confident and even convincing, but whether you accept it at face value depends entirely on you. Chances are that some aspects of the news are exaggerated, while others are absent altogether. Critical thinking enables you to get a clearer picture.

Finally, after all this work, you may want to take a vacation, say to a Greek island. As you've spent so much money on spare parts for the device you fixed, drinks with your problematic colleague (as you are now friends), and educational material on that new skill, you realize that this vacation needs to be budget-friendly too. Fortunately, there are plenty of options, especially if you decide on a quaint town in Crete. To help you make a satisfactory decision, you can apply critical thinking there as well.

Caveats of this framework

Thorough as this framework may be, just like any other critical thinking framework, it's not perfect. Knowing its limitations can help you utilize it better and possibly improve it.

First of all, the framework doesn't explore rhetoric and logical fallacies, which are still part of critical thinking. These come into play more in communication, but they still fall under this umbrella. Fortunately, they don't come into play as much in the context of data work, so you can still use this framework without any issues.

Additionally, the framework doesn't dwell on methodical thinking and strategizing, which are both important elements of critical thinking that manifest in certain scenarios of data work (for instance, when applying a new algorithm based on a research paper, or when developing a new kind of data product). Naturally, you can always add that in the information analysis and reflection part of the framework.

Moreover, the framework doesn't take into account your own experiences and skills, nor does it factor in time limitations. This is normal for every such framework, as they all aim to be as general as possible. Of course, you can always adapt the framework to your competencies and temporal constraints.

Finally, the framework isn't geared towards creativity, which can sometimes be integral to data work. We could include it as an additional stage, but this would rob the framework of its generality and make it more specialized for higher levels of thinking, which may not fit the context of data work.

Data work as a critical thinking process

As mentioned in Chapter 1, data work is closely linked to critical thinking (and communication). It's essentially an application of critical thinking to data, aimed at delivering value to the organization. In this sense, it's closely related to the data science process, which covers various stages of data transformation, turning it into more and more refined states. This process starts with gathering raw data (akin to the observation stage of the framework), cleaning and organizing it, and then interrogating it through hypotheses to better understand it (questioning stage). Next, the data, which has taken the form of a dataset (essentially quantified information), is analyzed using various data models, yielding deeper insights (information analysis stage). Then, the models are evaluated and the most useful one is selected. It's then used to gain deeper insights into the data and, in many cases, to develop data products (drawing conclusions stage). Throughout the process, the data scientist often goes back to previous stages as needed, armed with a better understanding of the data and its potential, strategizing more effectively and reviewing any assumptions made (reflection stage).

The insights and data products mentioned here can be viewed as specialized forms of the conclusions of a critical thinking process. Instead of being just logical deductions, they can be new facts inferred from the analysis and stand-alone applications that automate this transformation for new data. After all, they are conclusion-drawing in action, often for larger scales inaccessible to the human mind.

Data work often involves problem-solving since things don't go as planned. This can also be seen as a form of critical thinking in cases where information is convoluted and requires more analysis, deeper questioning, and additional reflection. Also, the engineering mindset is at the core of data work and closely connected to critical thinking.

Critical thinking in data work involves various aspects

Critical thinking is more clearly observed in specific aspects of data work. For example, in the engineering of a dataset, critical thinking comes into play when we gather the data, when we decide what parts to keep, when we combine the most relevant parts in a meaningful set (usually a table or a network of interconnected pieces of information), and when we explore the dataset through various hypotheses.

In building a data model, critical thinking comes into play as well. In this case, it guides us in selecting an appropriate set of models to try, in determining how to evaluate them for the problem at hand, and in selecting the optimal one. This may seem unnecessary to practitioners who just follow recipes, but data professionals with a better understanding of the field prefer the critical thinking approach. This extends to the maintenance of models once they are deployed as well.

Naturally, critical thinking is involved in other, more supplementary aspects of data work, such as data reporting and storytelling. However, in those cases, it's more of a supporting role, as communication takes on a primary role. It's hard to do them justice without a deeper understanding of the situation, the data, and the processes involved, all of which are made possible through critical thinking.

Critical thinking when developing a new pipeline

Critical thinking is also paramount when putting together a new data pipeline. Instead of keeping it a mechanical process prone to all kinds of issues, make it a conscious and deliberate act. Critical thinking comes into play when defining the pipeline requirements and how they are met, ensuring they are all relevant and feasible within the available resources. It is involved when the pipeline's structure is decided, optimizing it for the data at hand and the deliverables we seek. Critical thinking also plays an important role in automating the pipeline, anticipating potential pitfalls, and developing measures to address them. It's also the voice of reason that urges us to keep a human in the loop overseeing the whole pipeline when automation takes over. This is a key point, as it's not just about performance and KPIs but also about ensuring that people's data is managed properly and isn't made vulnerable because a malicious user bullies an LLM into deviating from its normal work.

Critical thinking is also key when maintaining the data pipeline. It helps us understand when it needs maintenance by focusing on relevant metrics and identifying the right ways to gather information from its users. And when the time comes to make the most challenging decision about the pipeline, such as whether to upgrade or deprecate, critical thinking ensures that we decide fairly and without prejudice. If we delve into it further, it can also guide us on how to upgrade it intelligently, rather than just mimicking other organizations on this matter.

The danger of overthinking

Critical thinking may be appealing, perhaps so much so that it becomes an end in and of itself. This leads to overthinking, which is a real issue sometimes. Let's think critically about all this.

First of all, critical thinking can be a time-consuming process when it lacks a clear scope. It's easy to get lost in the various thinking paths that unfold once you untangle a problem into its main threads. However, we don't have all the time in the world, nor all the cognitive resources often needed to pursue every avenue of reasoning. So, before we even enter the information analysis stage, it's good to define a clear, manageable scope to avoid the overthinking pitfall.

Sometimes, we may have a limited scope but still overthink, retracing the same paths to make sure everything is done perfectly. This may seem like diligence at first, but it's actually a form of perfectionism. To be productive, we need to combine critical thinking with action by instilling a sense of agency (executive energy). We are applying critical thinking not because it's comfortable, but because it enables us to minimize the time spent in discomfort, not avoid it altogether. This needs to become a realization and be accompanied by another essential quality of the critical thinker: courage, particularly the courage to act.

Finally, critical thinking can be a counterproductive endeavor when it's not accompanied by communication and ethical action. Just like the best data model in the world is useless without the right data (and the right amounts of it), critical thinking isn't of value when it's in a silo. The conclusions need to be communicated to the other people involved, and once an ethical course of action is found, take that action.

The role of ethics and action

As mentioned earlier, ethics and action grounded in critical thinking are a solution to the overthinking problem. Yet, they are more than that. Ethical action is also a great way to connect with the world in a more meaningful way. People care more about an organization's ethical standing now, and this approach can also be a key part of the organization's brand. Remember how OpenAI started and the success it got, partly because of this ethical/idealistic approach to AI.

Ethics can also serve as a balancing force when it comes to actions stemming from critical thinking. Not all avenues of action that are made available through the critical analysis of the facts are equally good. Some may be downright immoral and lack the subtler elements that make an action viable in the long term. So, even if we'd like to make decision-making as fact-based as possible, it's always good to balance it with a sense of morality that would ensure the organization isn't regretful a few steps down the line.

Additionally, ethics brings about a more harmonious approach to action. It's not just about the KPIs and following rigid logical processes and conclusions. It's also about addressing the more qualitative aspects of the situation and doing what's right. This is especially important when that's not the popular choice. For example, instead of going for the black-box approach to AI, you can opt for more transparent solutions.

Leveling up strategies

The idea of a meta-cognitive journal is based on an interview with Dr. Pearlman (*Breakthrough Brand* podcast). However, it's not like the journals most people keep for emotional hygiene and venting. Instead, it involves the in-depth analysis of a decision you've made and exploration of that cognitive space, including the various options available and their evaluation. It's a great opportunity to practice detachment, especially when using expressions like "my brain decided on X or Y" and examining the whole matter as an objective observer. The journal doesn't need to be daily, but it has a compounding effect, and it gets easier over time. In data work, it's particularly applicable to high-stakes decisions and very useful in challenging life situations in general. Naturally, as with any journal, reviewing your entries periodically is important to get the full benefit it offers. We'd highly recommend this strategy to anyone serious about critical thinking. We talk more about journaling in Chapter 6, in the context of effective communication.

This next strategy involves an age-old practice for developing critical thinking and overall mental prowess. It may not seem particularly challenging, but given how commonplace essay writing is in higher education, maybe there is more to it than giving educators additional work off campus. Essay-writing, when done properly, involves some research, too, and even though that's fairly easy today, it's not as easy as it may seem. When everyone and their dog has a professional-looking site, a podcast, or even a (self-published) book, it's hard to discern what's reliable information and what are the ramifications of questionable content. Considering the number of distractions and cognitive offloading tools out there these days, essay writing is best done offline (without the use of any offline AIs either). This may be more challenging but also more beneficial. But it can pay more dividends overall, as a strategy, as it's a great tool for learning, too.

Analyzing debates and information-rich talks is another strategy worth considering. This kind of content is the most useful for assimilation and practice. We are not talking about random podcasts or venting videos, but conversations or monologues of people who either do this for a living or have ample experience in public speaking. This strategy is best for cases where the content is on a topic you can follow, ideally structured to make it easier to understand. It also involves using a notebook or a note-taking application, as it can be challenging to retain all the ideas and concepts put forward for analysis later. Ideally, this strategy would be done in real time to improve focus (which generally enhances cognitive aptitude). You can always come back to the content afterward if there is a recording available, as it's often the case. This strategy can be a good first step for essay writing if you need inspiration and a great resource for learning.

Acting responsibly/ethically is a beneficial strategy not just for critical thinking but for any ability (for instance, communication). It's particularly essential for situations involving other people, especially if PII is present. Acting ethically enables dealing with more interesting challenges than the purely intellectual ones that are abundant in the data world. These are also the challenges that matter the most and are more than interesting topics to think about. Ethics is more of a compass for action, and ethical action is the only kind that can guarantee long-term benefits. In part, when it comes to data work, it's related to dealing with biases, confidentiality, etc., topics that many people are familiar with but fail to prioritize. Naturally, it heavily involves communication, too, as it's next to impossible without a team effort that involves collaboration at different levels and across different teams. We'll cover this topic in more detail in the next chapter.

Adopting a growth mindset is a great way to improve in general, and critical thinking is a great place to start. You don't have to be a self-improvement fanatic or a loyal follower of an influencer of this lifestyle either. Growth mindset is more subtle than that and is a way of thinking and living that's geared towards getting better over time, in various aspects of our lives (for instance, through healthy living and good educational practices). It's hard to keep up with the evolution of data work without such a mindset present. A sustainable mindset like this is closely linked to critical thinking, as the latter enables better discernment and strategy. Additionally, this growth mindset brings about a more visceral experience to the development of critical thinking, making it much more than an intellectual endeavor. If you think about it, it's more like the operating system of our minds, not just another app that may not make it till next year. The growth mindset is important not just for you as an individual but also for the organization as a whole, and it can be part of its culture, especially in data-related matters.

Case study: The AI recruiting tool that favored men

Even if Amazon is one of the leading tech companies in the world, it can also make critical thinking errors. In this scenario, this company's experimental AI recruiting tool from 2018 was trained on resumes submitted over a 10-year period, most of which were submitted by men. The AI learned to downgrade resumes with words like "women's" (e.g., "women's chess club") and to penalize graduates from women's colleges. From this, it soon became evident that it wasn't the specific clubs or colleges that were problematic, but the gender of the candidates (at least in the AI system's eyes).

What went wrong?

Apparently, various factors came into play to make such a disaster possible. The AI system doesn't decide by itself to be partial towards one kind of group, so it's not an algorithmic issue. These kinds of situations are usually linked to biases inherited from the data used to train the system. Note that this issue isn't AI-specific either. If the same data were used to train a different kind of model, say an ensemble model using various classifiers, the results would have been very similar. The data used to train any system is therefore of paramount importance, and its quality is multifaceted. You can't expect to have no issues just because there is plenty of data (even if large quantities often iron out biases that may exist in smaller datasets caused by sampling). If the original data is biased to start with, getting more of it will only make the biases more evident to the machine learning system trained on it.

Naturally, the company cannot be blamed for having had a biased approach to its hiring process. This bias may actually stem from the way the talent market has traditionally been, especially in the tech sector. The same bias could be found in resumes of candidates applying to Microsoft or Apple, for example. So, if we were to point fingers, they would be the people involved in getting the data from the data lake to the model, particularly those tasked with data preparation in the data science pipeline, as well as anyone leading them. Additionally, anyone who signed off on such a system upon its completion, simply because its KPIs looked good enough, should share some of the blame.

Digging deeper, it's becoming clearer that the issue is related to the decisions made about this data and to how the whole system was used, without any "sanity checks" during the production phase. It's not that the people involved were irresponsible; it's more likely that they were either rushing through this project or didn't appreciate the importance of carefully considering the factors involved and the consequences for end users before shipping this model into production.

How critical thinking could have saved the day

It turns out that this sort of situation could be easily remedied or even prevented by applying the aforementioned framework. If Chris Thomas (the critical thinking practitioner from the book's introduction) were in the data division of Amazon at that time, how would he handle the situation? Naturally, this depends on which stage of the problem he would get involved in.

If Chris Thomas had been around at the beginning of all this (for instance, by taking on the role of a PM or tech auditor), the whole problem could have been averted altogether. He would have checked the data (either on his own using a visualization tool) and observed the bias discrepancy, and brought it up in the next meeting. He would have alerted all the data scientists and AI engineers involved in this matter. He would have started a discussion on how it could be tackled (with questions like "What effects would this have on the end user?" and "How can we resolve this issue without delaying the product too much?"). Upon reflecting on the whole matter and incorporating the information the other stakeholders would bring to the table, he would analyze all the facts and explore different solutions. Then he would talk to the engineers once more, examining with them the feasibility of these solutions (for instance, balancing the resume counts between the different candidates based on their gender, synthesizing new data, using a more advanced model that takes bias into account, etc.). Then, he would reflect further and eventually draw conclusions on how they should proceed, discuss them in the next meeting, this time with everyone involved, and monitor the matter, ensuring that the shipped model would be up to the task without any gender prejudice built into it.

If Chris Thomas wasn't involved until later (in this case, he would be like a fixer or a consultant), then the situation would be more challenging but still salvageable. In this case, he would first observe the situation, assess the scale of the problem (damage control), and reflect on it, coming up with good questions to better understand it. Next, he would ask all the people involved in this for their views on the situation and examine how much each of them was responsible. Without pointing any fingers, he would then analyze the gathered information and reflect on it, trying to identify potential root causes. It wouldn't take him long to figure out that biased data was the culprit, so he would draw his conclusions and recommend how to proceed to fix the issue.

Chances are that the solutions would be similar to the ones he'd find in the previous scenario, though how they would be applied in this case would be somewhat different. Perhaps a new model would need to be built, or the AI system retrained (depending on the flexibility of the models used). Regardless, he would still monitor the issue and develop a checklist of items to check in the data to ensure this problem wouldn't arise again.

Key lessons

The key lessons from this case study are threefold:

- **Bias in Training Data**. AI reflects the biases in its training data. Critical thinking is needed to question the data's representativeness and audit for fairness.

- **Validation**. Always probe the decision with questions like *"What groups might be excluded or misrepresented in this dataset?"* and *"How would this bias affect the end user and the company as a result?"*

- **Action.** Amazon scrapped the tool, but the incident highlights the need for human oversight in AI systems, particularly in high-stakes situations.

What other lessons did you derive from this? Was your solution accurate? Remember to take notes and review them regularly to further hone your critical skills. Chris Thomas may be a fictional character, but what he represents is real and much needed in every data project and initiative.

Key takeaways

- Critical thinking is the active process of questioning assumptions, evaluating evidence over biases, and applying adaptable frameworks, especially in data-driven fields, to make better decisions. Recognize that frameworks are tools with limitations and should be tailored to context, such as integrating human and computational cognition, while balancing core abilities like analysis, inference, skepticism, and sensitivity to others.

- Critical thinking is a dynamic, non-linear process comprising five interconnected stages (observation, questioning, information analysis, concluding, and reflection), each building on the others and requiring practice, adaptability, and metacognition to effectively address problems and generate insights.

- Critical thinking is foundational to data work, framing it as a deliberate, iterative process (from gathering and cleaning data to analysis, modeling, and drawing actionable insights) while also guiding ethical decision-making, problem-solving, and pipeline development. Always watch out for overthinking, however.

- Leveling up critical thinking involves practical strategies like maintaining a meta-cognitive journal for self-reflection, writing essays to deepen analysis and research skills, analyzing structured debates or talks for real-time learning, acting ethically to address meaningful challenges, and adopting a growth mindset to foster continuous personal and professional improvement.

- The need for human oversight in AI systems is directly linked to the use of critical thinking. This includes both the system design **and** the data used to train it. A question-driven approach to gathering the necessary facts and a careful examination of them are key to resolving problems in such systems, particularly when they are not obvious.

CHAPTER 5

Ethics and Bias in Practice

"Ethics is knowing the difference between what you have a right to do and what is right to do."

Potter Stewart

We briefly touched on ethics throughout this book. Although it deserves a book of its own, we'll try to do it justice in this chapter before we continue our journey to the communication part of the book. Much of the drama in data work could be alleviated if ethics were given the attention it deserves. Overall, ethics is a strong regulator and a compass of sorts when it comes to making hard decisions about data products and how we implement data science within an organization. Nowadays, it's mostly about the use of AI, as that's where ethics comes into play most. AI is still quite unpredictable for the most part, and its influence on people cannot be overstated. Ethics helps keep tabs on that and ensure we can at least foresee and tackle some of the issues it raises. It's noteworthy to make a distinction between Ethical AI (which is more high-level) and Responsible AI (which is more like the implementation of ethics when developing and deploying an AI system). Naturally, the latter wouldn't exist without the former and with an ethical approach to data in general.

Ethics in data work (especially when AI is leveraged) involves different aspects, with bias being a key one (other verticals include privacy and accountability). Most of that falls under the data governance umbrella, though bias trickles down to analytics to a large extent as well. Based on a meta-analysis of articles in the healthcare industry on AI ethics, algorithmic and data bias are by far the most important concerns (Figure 11[12]).

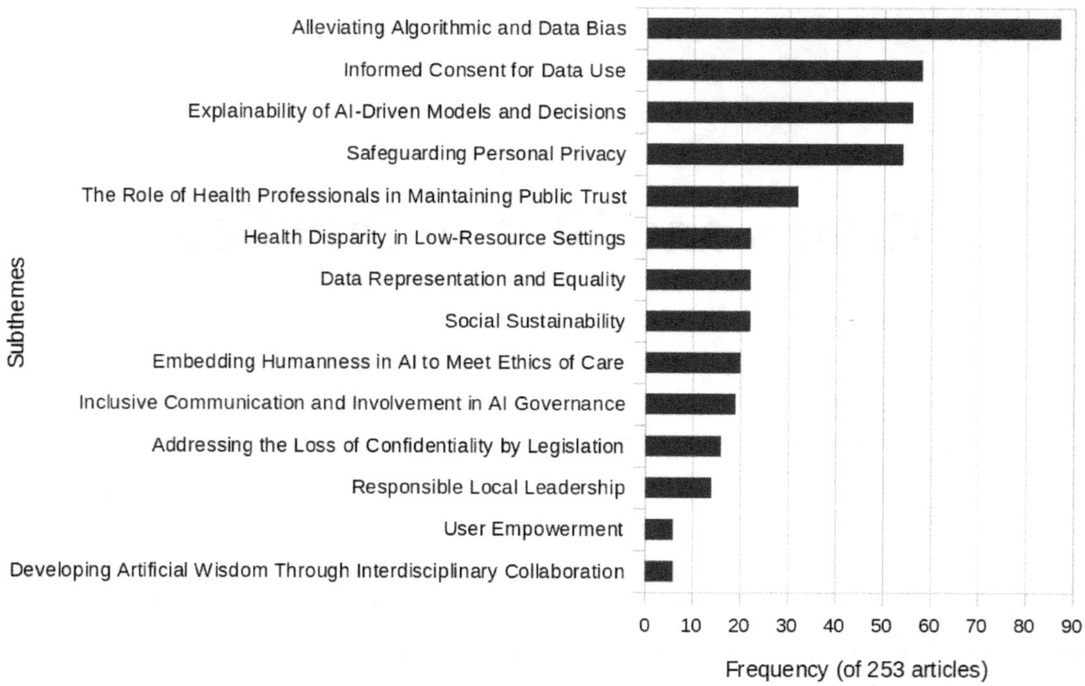

Figure 11: Subthemes in AI ethics literature and their frequencies (based on research published in mid 2025).

This is not an issue only in that industry, however. According to a 2025 study in the World Journal of Advanced Research and Reviews, "addressing algorithmic bias is imperative to ensure fair and ethical decision making," while The Journal of Information, Communication and Ethics in Society (also in 2025) makes the point that purely technical solutions are insufficient. It advocates a socio-technical framework that includes stakeholder engagement, participatory design, and governance approaches to comprehensively address bias. Beyond facts and figures, however, there is also a need for qualitative research on this topic, something the AI and ethics literature review emphasized (2025). For example, case studies, interviews, and related materials are crucial for understanding the contextual and strategic aspects of bias, alongside technical fixes. In other words, the ethics of AI

---

12 based on the chart in the article: https://pmc.ncbi.nlm.nih.gov/articles/PMC11977975

(and other aspects of data work) is broad and manifests in various ways, with bias being the most prevalent example.

Biases are inevitable in modern datasets, especially when they arise from combining different data streams.

However, it's often inevitable that we'll notice them at one point. The challenge is to do so early in the pipeline, so we can address them before they become a serious problem. The latter occurs when they become part of an automated process, usually stemming from a data project, whether an AI system or a dashboard.

Navigating biases is key in data work, as it makes or breaks the end result, especially when it's a customer-facing system. As they are more common than other ethics-related issues, we'll take a closer look at them later in this chapter. Besides, this kind of bias is one we can do more about and are most likely to be held responsible for. Considering how AI tends to magnify these kinds of issues, it's not just an important but also an urgent matter.

Interestingly, about 77% of companies with bias-testing protocols still found active bias after implementation, often because testing occurs post-deployment rather than during model training.[13] This insight not only shows the gravity of bias in the world but also how it's directly linked to an attitude problem and ethics.

There is no doubt that every data project can improve in quality by handling its key aspects (for instance, biases) ethically, rather than chasing deadlines. This becomes more apparent in large-scale operations, such as data initiatives. It's not enough to have a good set of features in the projects involved; you also need to adhere to ethical guidelines and manage biases diligently.

---

[13] www.allaboutai.com/resources/ai-statistics/ai-bias (October 2025)

The 4 R's of ethics in data work and where critical thinking and communication fit

To better visualize ethics and its relationship to data work, we developed a mnemonic framework that encapsulates its most relevant qualities. The latter comprises four key ethical aspects related to any data project or initiative. These are Respect (for the people involved), Reputation, Revision, and Responsibility (see Figure 12 for more context). The order of these R's isn't particularly important. What is important is that we consider them in every data project and ensure we don't get trapped in the bubble of our day-to-day work, detaching ourselves from the end result.

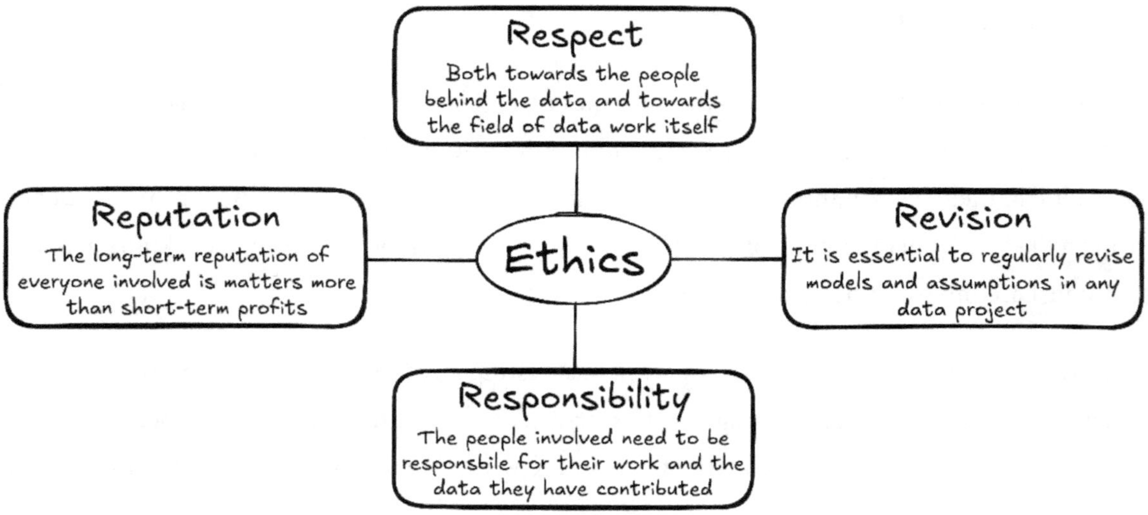

Figure 12: The four R's of ethics in data work.

Note that the 4 R's cover all areas of data work, not just the challenging parts, such as biases. However, the more we embody these verticals in our planning and mindset, the better the chances of tackling bias-related issues before they manifest. Also, the 4 R's address other issues, such as the privacy and accountability issues mentioned earlier. These are addressed in the respect and responsibility aspects of ethics, respectively. Regardless, all 4 R's need to work together, as only then do they bring about a shift in mindset and enable a more sustainable kind of action.

Much like the other frameworks covered in this book, this one works best when all its aspects work together. It's hard to act ethically if you don't care about the organization's reputation, for example. If you aren't sure where exactly to incorporate ethics into your workflow, you can address it at the beginning and briefly circle back to it at the end. Even though ethics (as action) tends to be the end result of a work process, it also needs to be a guiding principle. As such, it permeates all other aspects of the workflow.

Critical thinking comes into play mainly through the revision and responsibility aspects of ethics. When implementing an ethical initiative, critical thinking is paramount, which is why we discussed it in length in the previous chapter. Note that critical thinking needs to be anchored somewhere for it to be more effective. Otherwise, it's easy to fall into one of its pitfalls, such as overthinking and never completing the cycle in a meaningful timeframe. Also, when initiating your critical thinking process, it's much more profound when it uses revision and responsibility as a starting point.

Communication mainly comes into play in matters of respect and reputation. Again, when implementing an ethical initiative, communication is paramount as it connects the dots, making a network out of otherwise isolated nodes. In essence, it does with people what critical thinking does with information. However, for alignment between these two processes, ethics needs to be firmly established in the workflow. Communication can happen in different ways, and it's very easy to get lured into a more shallow form that focuses on tactics rather than long-term strategy. Communication needs to be deep, and this depth can only come from a sense of ethics.

The 4 I's of bias in data work and where critical thinking and communication fit

This is another mnemonic rule to help make the whole bias matter more concrete, eliminating any potential biases around it. We often think of bias as a single thing, usually discrimination against a particular minority group. However, it can take different forms and goes beyond demographic data. The mental model we propose here comprises four distinct verticals that cover a wide range of datasets across the majority of use cases. These are what we refer to as the 4 I's of bias, namely Imbalance (in the sizes of the data categories involved), Incomplete feature sets, Inadequate connections with the real world (for instance, ideological biases), and Insufficient understanding of the models involved (Figure 13).

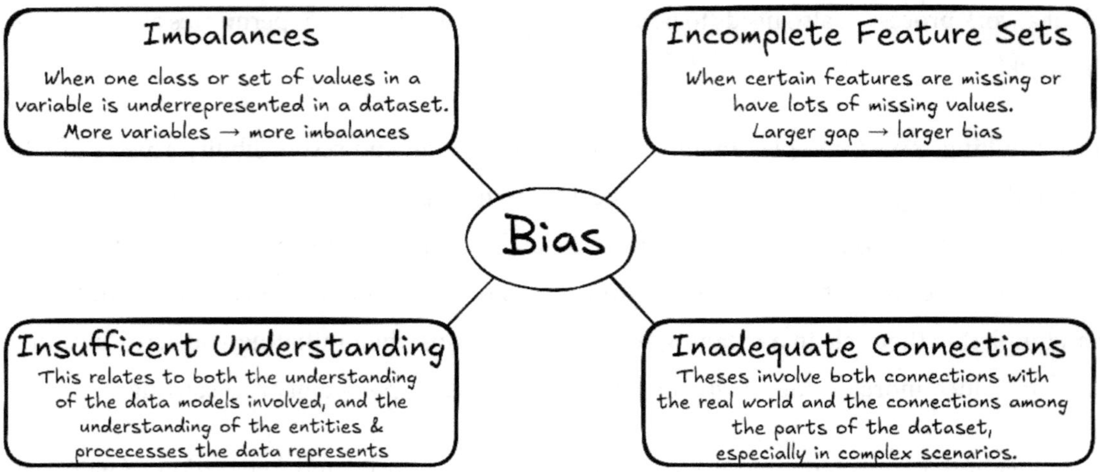

Figure 13: The four I's of bias usually encountered in data work.

The 4 I's of bias are particularly evident in AI-related products, given the large amounts of data involved and the complexity of the models. Their opacity only amplifies the issue, making biases more subtle and harder to detect until it's already too late. The unpredictability of AI systems also makes testing them very time-consuming, resulting in products that haven't been thoroughly tested and that exhibit a variety of biases. Coupled with the fact that most people doing AI these days lack the understanding of data work that more traditional data professionals have, this bias issue only gets worse over time.

Fortunately, critical thinking helps to some extent. When it's by itself, it may not be able to tackle these verticals of bias, but it can at least help identify them and sometimes suggest potential solutions regarding them, for the project at hand. The problem with biases is that they are often deep-seated and tough to change, much like an organization's culture (and often related to it). You can't just think your way out of bias, especially if it's already ingrained in the data at hand. However, when applied properly, critical thinking can be a good starting point.

Similarly, communication alone cannot address these aspects of bias either. However, it can help ensure that everyone is on the same page about them and gradually build consensus on how to address bias in the project at hand. This can help explore potential solutions identified by critical thinking. It is important to go deep into the issues, though, exploring different viewpoints and getting to the crux of the problems. If the way we collect data is flawed, biases will persist even if we remedy the datasets we are working with now. So, a long-term solution needs to be found, something that may involve multiple people brainstorming on this issue. Otherwise, we may just opt for a patch that fixes the problem only partially and only for the current project.

Although ethics is a more general ability that is not fully equipped to resolve biases, it can be a key aspect of the whole process. It brings about a mindset shift that enables you to persist more when exploring solutions, go deeper in understanding the problem, and connect better with the people involved. The solution won't come about through the next big AI model or through some miracle process put forward by a business or tech guru. By employing respect for the people involved (especially those who get discriminated against in the data product), revision of the assumptions made and the model in general, responsibility in how you manage the whole bias issue, and care for the reputation of your organization, you are bound to go further towards a solution and its implementation.

Some noteworthy tools for checking and handling biases in ML and AI models are *AIFairness360* (IBM), *Fairlearn* (Microsoft), and *What-If Tool* (Google). These tools are widely used across industries like finance, healthcare, and hiring to address ethical and social challenges related to algorithmic bias. Research indicates that applying mitigation algorithms sequentially across the machine learning lifecycle (pre-processing, in-processing, and post-processing) can be more effective than using a single stage in isolation. While AIF360 is often preferred for its extensive algorithmic suite, Fairlearn is favored for its simplicity and visualization capabilities, while the What-If Tool serves best for interactive model diagnosis rather than direct bias correction.

Other ethical frameworks and regulations

Beyond the hands-on framework we discussed, which directly applies to data work, there are others with a more established role in the field. You may already be familiar with them to some extent, but it doesn't hurt to mention them here and look at how they affect our work.

Overarching ethical frameworks

The two main overarching frameworks that define our ethical actions are *utilitarianism* and *deontology*. The first one is all about utility (hence the name) while the second is all about what we ought to do (from the Greek δεοντολογία).

Utilitarianism is based on the idea that an action is morally right if it maximizes overall happiness or reduces suffering for the greatest number of people. This may seem very scientific and appeal to the quant aspect of us, but in practice, it's extremely hard to measure these matters objectively. Additionally, this approach to ethics tends to be harsh towards minorities. On the plus side, it's very practical, at least until problems arise from it. A simple example of this framework is sacrificing one person's privacy (for instance, sharing their data without consent) to develop a life-saving AI model for millions, which is justifiable under the utilitarian framework. Most AI labs today operate with this philosophy.

Deontology is founded upon the idea that actions are morally right if they adhere to duties or rules, regardless of consequences. It's all about intentions and steadfast rules, such as "respect autonomy" and "never lie," that provide clear moral boundaries. However, it can be quite rigid and lead to morally debatable outcomes if these rules are followed blindly (i.e., without critical thinking). A clear example of deontology in practice is the case where, even if lying would save lives, someone would argue it's wrong because honesty is a moral duty.

Naturally, there is no clear winner here, but pondering these matters and challenging yourself with different ways of thinking about ethical issues can help you develop a more robust ethical identity and a better understanding of others who may follow a different ethical framework. Also, it may help the regulatory standards affecting data work make more sense.

Regulatory standards

Nowadays, there is a plethora of standards for data work, particularly in data governance and data acquisition. Some are EU-specific, while others are focused on the US. The main ones are the following:

- **General Data Protection Regulation (GDPR)**. This is an EU-related regulation that's been around for a few years now. However, it's not limited to companies in EU countries; it involves any company around the world that deals with EU citizens, ensuring that any data related to them is acquired only with their explicit consent. So, even if you work in a company on the other side of the world, as long as it deals with data related to people with EU citizenship, this regulation applies to you.

- **Digital Operational Resilience Act (DORA)**. This is another EU-related piece of legislation that mandates stringent requirements for data storage, access, and security in the financial services sector within the EU. It aims to ensure that financial entities can withstand, respond to, and recover from all types of ICT-related disruptions and threats. Since financial data is among the most sensitive kinds of data we deal with, it's good to be aware of this regulation, especially when operating in EU countries.

- **Health Insurance Portability and Accountability Act (HIPAA)**. This US-based legislation sets the standard for protecting sensitive patient data nationwide. It requires healthcare organizations to implement safeguards to ensure the confidentiality, integrity, and availability of protected health information (PHI), which is probably the most sensitive kind of PII. Naturally, this regulation primarily affects MedTech companies and similar entities.

- **Fair Credit Reporting Act (FCRA).** This is another US-based law that regulates the collection, accuracy, and use of consumer credit information. Additionally, it gives consumers the right to access their credit reports and dispute inaccuracies. This law requires credit reporting agencies to ensure the information they provide is fair and accurate.

Beyond these, several others are either more general or narrower in scope, such as the California Consumer Privacy Act (CCPA) and California Privacy Rights Act (CPRA), which apply to people living in California, and the Gramm-Leach-Bliley Act (GLBA), which is the DORA equivalent for the U.S.

AI-specific ethical standards

AI has its own set of ethical standards that require special attention. The most important of these are:

- **Algorithm Accountability Act (AAA).** This is a proposed U.S. federal law to regulate automated decision systems (ADS) and AI, ensuring transparency, fairness, and accountability. However, at the time of this writing, this is not yet an active federal law, as it remains a proposed bill in the U.S. Congress. One can hope that it will one day pass and help regulate the AI companies in Silicon Valley and other parts of the country.

- **EU AI Act**. This is the latest EU legislation on data processing, with a focus on AI-related systems and the data they use. At the time of this writing, it's partially applied, with full force coming into effect by August 2027. If you are operating in the EU, you must be familiar with this regulatory framework.

- **IEEE Ethically Aligned Design**. This framework focuses on human well-being, accountability, and transparency across the entire AI lifecycle. It emphasizes the involvement of all stakeholders, including end users and those affected by AI systems, and provides detailed guidance on governance, due diligence, and operational procedures. In essence, it's like a manual for designing and building ethical AI systems.

- **OECD AI Principles**. Adopted in 2019 and updated in 2024, these principles promote human-centric AI development, emphasizing fairness, transparency, robustness, security, and accountability. They are designed to guide both policy-makers and AI developers in creating trustworthy AI systems.

If you are interested in learning more about these frameworks and their implications in AI use and development, you can check out the book *AI Safety: Strategies for Ensuring Responsible, Ethical, and Reliable AI Systems* (Technics Publications) published recently, where all these matters are discussed in details without any legalese and with many practical examples of how an ethical (and relatively safe) AI system can exist.

Leveling up on ethics

Let's now look at how you can level up your ethics with a focus on action in your data-related work. The first strategy involves acting responsibly/ethically when developing and testing both critical thinking and communication, and going beyond them. In other words, we need to have ethical action as a goal whenever we improve critical thinking or communication. A void of ethics, communication, and critical thinking can devolve into sophistry and manipulation devices.

Additionally, you can try to be more attentive to signs of bias in the data and in the models you build. Some biases are inevitable, but it's usually the more provocative ones that create issues. Even if you don't eliminate biases from a dataset or a model, you can still improve it enough to mitigate or even eliminate the damage they would otherwise cause. Being conscious of them will enable you to identify them sooner and even tackle them proactively, to the extent your role allows.

Challenging data strategy decisions whenever there is user backlash is another strategy you can employ to strengthen your ethics. This may seem like a responsibility you naturally assume. Still, you'd be surprised how many people choose to look the other way to avoid stirring the waters, mainly out of fear or complacency. However, dealing with an inaccurate decision in a data strategy is far easier and less painful than dealing with the consequences. This is especially true if it involves a new product or service that affects the lives of many customers or users.

Furthermore, thinking more long-term about the systems built and deployed goes hand in hand with ethics. Long-term thinking is equivalent to proper planning, beyond the rigid and often limited time frames of most data projects. Ethics doesn't care about the next quarter or the next year; it's more concerned with long-term well-being. This not only leads to better decisions but also helps you be more aligned with customers, even if the latter aren't fully aware of it. It is a very active process, too, as it involves getting out of the usual thinking patterns, reflecting on them, engaging with them, and being proactive about a data project or initiative in ways others are not. Privacy-focused platforms have embodied this mindset, and they needn't be the only ones, either. There is plenty of room for improvement in all kinds of organizations when it comes to involving a more ethical approach to data, going beyond keeping PII safe.

Finally, it's always advisable to uphold ethical values within the team/department /organization and to adhere to them in both planning and actions. Good values inspire others to do their best and often go beyond what's expected. They bring about a better culture, one that naturally gravitates towards good products, solid decisions, and better quality in every aspect of the data pipeline, be it in handling biases, constructing meaningful datasets, or building models that empower users instead of exploiting their weaknesses.

Case study: The AI that prioritized wealthy patients

A healthcare AI tool, RoboDoc, was introduced by a startup, aiming to revolutionize diagnostics via AI on the web. The system was trained on a large database of patients, licensed from an insurance company. Although RoboDoc was open to everyone, it was found to favor wealthier, white patients for specialized care because it used healthcare costs as a proxy for need (wealthier patients had higher historical costs).

What went wrong?

The AI was clearly biased towards this particular demographic and discriminated against everyone else. It didn't take long for users to become outraged and threaten to sue the company for discrimination. As a result, there was significant churn among non-favored customers, and the reviews reflected this negative sentiment. Naturally, the investors were not too happy about it either, and the company had a hard time securing additional funding. The fact that the company wasn't even aware of the problem until users pointed it out only made matters worse, adding to the overall tension.

How ethics saved the day

The ethics committee assembled and reviewed the problem, with the help of Chris Thomas and other advisors. Eventually, they dissected the issue and identified key bias verticals, primarily in the data. This included clear class imbalances across different user types, a lack of in-depth features (such as HRV-based ones) that complemented demographic profiles, an evidently inadequate connection to real-world users, and a fairly insufficient understanding of exactly how the AI system worked.

By first focusing on users and listening to their concerns, they identified which demographic segments actually used the system and how under-represented they were in the dataset used for the AI's training. They then revised their assumptions about who their target audience was and sought additional data to retrain the system. The data was more balanced and included additional features that were more universal than those in the original dataset. The company assumed responsibility for the problem and issued a public statement to that effect. A PR specialist was hired to help get on top of the matter and repair the company's reputation. Eventually, the whole issue was spun positively, showing how flexibility, adaptability, and empathy were key values of the company, not just in theory but in practice. Finally, they thoroughly tested the revised model and ensured it was as fair as possible before releasing it to the public.

Through all these ethics-driven actions, the whole tension with the unhappy users was defused. Gradually, the issue settled peacefully without involving attorneys. The whole matter became a valuable learning experience that helped the company prevent similar problems in the future.

Key lessons

From this example, we can derive the following lessons:

- **Ethical Blind Spots**. AI can optimize for the wrong objectives if not guided by ethical principles. Understanding and respecting the end-user was necessary, aligned with the system's reality, and the data used to train it.

- **Stakeholder Impact**. Asking questions like "Who might be harmed by this model's decisions?" would help stay one step ahead of the matter and be proactive, showing both responsibility and care for the company's reputation.

- **Advocacy**. Data teams must push back when AI outcomes conflict with ethical values. Revision here is key, as the data products (for instance, AI systems) need to align with reality rather than the other way around.

- Based on all the ethical matters we discussed, what's one ethical strategy you'd pick to incorporate in your workflow in the next week/month/quarter?

Key takeaways

- Ethics in data work serves as a crucial regulator, especially for unpredictable AI, guiding decisions and mitigating issues such as bias (human, algorithmic, and data), privacy, and accountability. Bias is a pervasive challenge across industries that must be addressed early to prevent systemic problems and ensure responsible, high-quality outcomes.
- The 4 R's framework (Respect, Reputation, Revision, Responsibility) serves as a mnemonic to embed ethics into every data project, ensuring holistic consideration of users, proactive bias and privacy management, critical thinking, and meaningful communication. In this framework, all elements are working together to foster a sustainable, ethical mindset throughout the workflow.
- The 4 I's of bias (Imbalance, Incomplete feature sets, Inadequate real-world connections, and Insufficient model understanding) highlight systemic biases in data work, amplified by AI, data scale, model complexity, and lack of traditional data expertise. Tackling them requires critical thinking, open communication, and ethical commitment (respect, revision, responsibility, care) to address both immediate and deep-seated issues, as superficial fixes risk perpetuating biases.
- You can level up ethics in data work by integrating ethical action into critical thinking and communication, proactively addressing biases in data and models, challenging questionable data strategies, adopting a long-term perspective on system impacts, and embedding ethical values in team culture to drive better decisions and user-centric outcomes.

- Ethical AI Development is a good example of ethics in practice. AI systems risk optimizing for misaligned objectives without clear ethical guidance; teams must proactively assess potential harms to stakeholders, advocate for ethical alignment over flawed outcomes, and ensure that the data and models underlying them reflect real-world values and impacts.

Overarching Ethical Frameworks:

- Utilitarianism focuses on maximizing overall happiness or reducing suffering for the greatest number, which is practical but can overlook minority rights.
- Deontology emphasizes adhering to moral duties and rules (for instance, honesty, respect for autonomy) regardless of consequences, providing clear boundaries but potentially leading to rigid outcomes.

Key Regulatory and AI-Specific Standards:

- **Regulatory Standards.** GDPR (global data privacy), DORA (EU financial data resilience), HIPAA (U.S. healthcare data), FCRA (U.S. credit data), CCPA/CPRA (California consumer privacy), and GLBA (U.S. financial data).
- **AI-Specific Standards.** EU AI Act (phased implementation by 2027), IEEE Ethically Aligned Design (human-centric AI governance), OECD AI Principles (fairness, transparency, accountability), and the proposed U.S. Algorithmic Accountability Act (transparency and fairness in AI).

CHAPTER 6

Getting Communication Right

"The limits of my language are the limits of my world."

Ludwig Wittgenstein

According to the Shannon-Weaver model (see Chapter 1), we only have control over our side of the communication, the intended message, the chosen channel, and our capability in translating our message into the right format for the channel. The message is the content we choose: which facts, which conclusions, which caveats. The transmitter is how we encode that content into language, visuals, and structure. The channel is the medium we select: a dashboard, a written note, a workshop, or a Slack thread. Effective communication in data work starts from the assumption that our leverage lies in deliberately designing these three elements.

In this chapter, we want to provide you with a mental framework for creating comprehensible and convincing communication, regardless of your chosen medium. We will focus on the conversations in the data world, but this approach will likely be helpful in any context.

Why communication in data feels noisy

Data work is communication in a permanently noisy environment. Metrics shift names over time, dashboards multiply, and stakeholders arrive with very different levels of literacy and context. Even when the numbers are correct, the message often does not land, a carefully prepared analysis degenerates into a debate about definitions, or a critical risk is buried in slide 27 of a deck no one reads. From a distance, this looks like a technical problem. Up close, it is mostly a communication problem; the signal we intended to send is distorted by noise long before it reaches the decision it was supposed to influence.

As shown by the examples above, the noise is often self-created, a part of the process of analyzing and sharing data and its related insights. So to increase our chances of getting the key points across, we not only have to bring clarity to our message but also ensure minimal noise. The latter is only partly in our control, but at the very least, we can stop adding to the noise. Surrounding noise from the rest of the organization, the recipient's schedule, and general business conditions are beyond our control. But with a growing use of critical thinking, for instance, as lived by data people like you, we can support our recipients in separating signal from noise.

Providing CLEAR communication

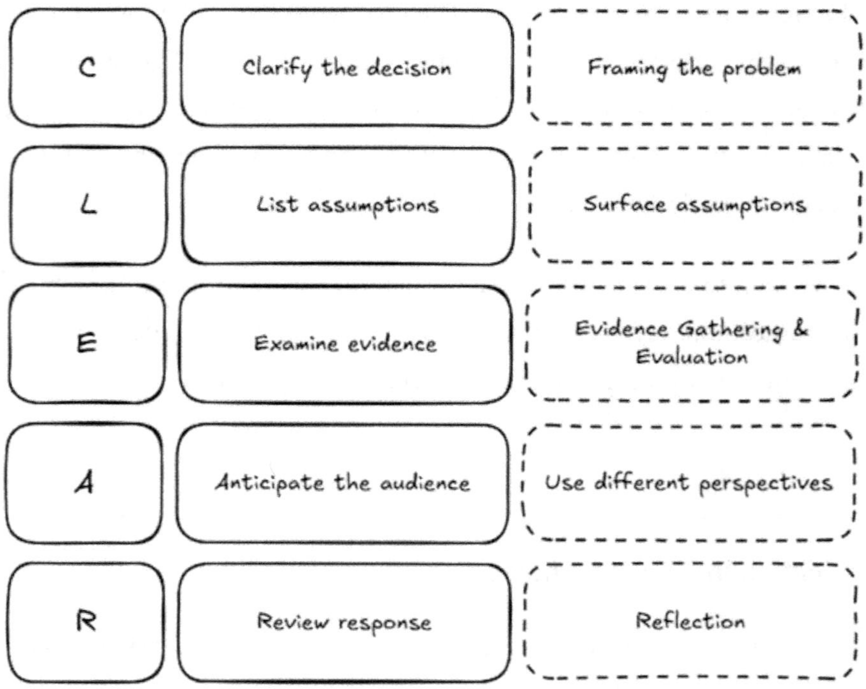

Figure 14: CLEAR mnemonic for communication.

With our knowledge about communication (Chapter 1) and Critical Thinking (Chapter 4), we can create a simple scheme to base our communication on. We will call it CLEAR, for obvious reasons. With it, we will cover the message and the transmission. The medium is intentionally left out, as this is not always within our control, depending on organizational or technical requirements. But thanks to the COVID pandemic and its required switch to remote work, a myriad of ways were found to translate many physical media into the digital realm. At the same time, digital tools have become easier to use, so that anyone can, for instance, create their own narrated and animated recordings.

Clarify the decision

Within critical thinking, we learned about the importance of framing the problem. We translate this into "clarifying the decision to be made" within the context of our data world. Data is ultimately about making decisions, whether for questions we already had, for questions that arise from an interesting finding, or for automating decisions via data-based technology.

So, within our communication, not just the preceding data work, we have to emphasize which decision we are talking about. This includes making sure that our audience, our recipients, are connected to and ideally responsible and able to make the decision. This may sound straightforward, but in times of 50+ people on video calls or sharing slides and documents with half of one's organization, restraint is becoming a new superpower. Interestingly, this broad distribution of information becomes part of the organization's background noise.

Equally important is the context in which the decision is to be made. So we also state all relevant facts surrounding the decision. Examples include existing policies, strategies, legal requirements, or the organization's values.

List assumptions

Again, we will outline the assumptions underlying the decisions to be made, as we did at the start of the analysis. This provides a common ground for all recipients regarding the context under which the following information is to be understood.

The following aspects can be part of this section of your "signal":

- Known external and internal factors influencing the decision, for instance, time constraints
- Prior analyses or decisions relevant to this decision
- Known or expected consequences
- Definition of all metrics used (or referenced) within this document.

As we can see, this section of the document can become lengthy. Ideally, we only reference existing documentation and do not need to copy anything into the current medium. The potential length also provides a reason to distribute your report, in whatever form, earlier so that recipients have enough time to become familiar with the context.

Examine evidence

This is the core of our message, the evidence, and the conclusion leading to the decision. Here, we create the narrative based on the insights we discovered in our analysis. Such a narrative can take many forms, from drill-downs and drill-throughs with minimalist line charts to complex interactive visuals to interspersed customer interviews; anything is possible.

What we are aiming for is creating a story. A story is more than just a sequence of statistics; it is a combination of imagery, affect, and attention. Or, in other words, a small journey with a satisfying outcome. Studies show that stories stick way better with audiences than just the facts.[14]

The rule of thumb for any element you add should be, Does this add to the narrative? Or is it just a side-story, or a different perspective on the same aspect we already covered? Minimalism is key. In the amount of elements we use, the different kinds of elements we present, and the design of the individual elements. A commonly misinterpreted study from 1956 claims that humans can hold "seven, plus or minus two" items in working memory, but more recent reviews by Nelson Cowan establish the limit closer to four chunks.[15] We need to consider this when creating the storyline. It may contain more steps, but the last four need to be connected in a meaningful way.

---

14 Thomas Graeber, Christopher Roth, Florian Zimmermann "Stories, Statistics, and Memory", 2024

15 Nelson Cowan "The Magical Number 4 in Short-Term Memory", 2001

A great guideline for designing individual visuals in your story is the data-ink ratio, or the concept of data ink by Edward Tufte. It aims to maximize the share of "ink" used for actual data rather than clutter, also known as supporting elements. An example is to highly discourage the use of duplicate data labels, which are either on the axis or on the line or bar.

Something to accompany any evidence are notes about the underlying data quality or uncertainty involved in the data work. This should not become a list of grievances or an indirect pitch to disregard any of the insights given, but a reminder that certainty is hard to come by in a complex reality. Equally, contradictory evidence should be acknowledged. This supports our approach to emphasizing critical thinking. So, presenting counterexamples enables our audience to better engage with the data and increases our credibility by showing that we considered the alternatives.

The final step goes back to the decision outlined at the beginning. Depending on the organization's decision-making processes, this can be the point at which the decision is made.

Anticipate the audience

Besides ensuring that we address the right people with the right information, we need to address them in the right way. The right wording, the right level of detail, the right balance between visuals and text, and the right story. But what is right? That depends on our audience. We can ask ourselves, what do they already know, what do they care about, and what constraints and fears do they have? Using this, we can decide what to include, what to omit, which language to use, and how to structure our message so it is understandable and actionable for them, not just correct for us.

> *Even the perfect visual we created in the previous step, or the most magnificent insight, can fail to land if we are unable to move from our reasoning into the audience's mental model.*

Here are some considerations that will guide the final shape of our signal:

Knowledge level:

- What concepts are unfamiliar to them?
- Which terms must we define explicitly (for instance, "active user", "churn", "conversion")?

- Where can we safely skip details?

Goals and incentives:

- What does success look like for them (not us)?
- How does our recommendation connect to their KPIs, risks, or narrative?

Constraints:

- **Time**: how much attention do they realistically have for this message?
- **Format**: is this a slide, a Slack message, a steering committee decision paper?
- **Decision rights**: are they the decision-maker, an advisor, or an implementer?

Emotional landscape:

- Are we challenging someone's work, pet metric, or strategy?
- Is there likely defensiveness, fear, or status anxiety we need to account for?
- Do we need to open with appreciation, context, or reassurance?

The latter section may be the most surprising part for data work. But it is the most relevant as we are dealing with humans, as humans. Decisions are rarely based on pure fact but on underlying emotions. Emotions can influence decision making in two ways: integral and incidental.[16] Integral means the emotion is relevant to the decision, like fear about a risky investment. Incidental refers to unrelated emotions, like a bad mood due to the weather. The latter is again outside our control, but we can address the integral factors. This can be done by pointing out uncertainties.

Review response

Our communication does not end with sending it out or with a decision. We anticipate and even request a response. Did the audience understand the reasoning, and did they act on it? Did the decision produce the expected change in behavior or metrics, or did new problems appear?

These steps serve two purposes: improving our communication by checking the received message and evaluating our critical thinking. Just as in the reflection step of the critical thinking process, we

16See Västfall et. al. "The Arithmetic of Emotion: Integration of Incidental and Integral Affect in Judgments and Decisions", 2016

can review whether the assumptions we made at the beginning are correct and complete. If they are not, we update them and use the revised version for the next data work in the same area. Equally, we check whether the evidence was appropriate and convincing, and whether the expected outcomes match the anticipated ones. This may seem like overkill, since our initial goal was to support the decision that has likely already happened. But without reviewing our methods, we will repeat them unquestioningly the next time we are tasked with similar work. Over time, this approach will lead to iterative improvements, forming a learning loop.

If our organization lacks a formal follow-up process, we can create our own simple feedback loop. After a reasonable amount of time (for instance, two weeks), we send out a brief, 3-question email to the key decision-maker:

1. Looking back, was the information we provided clear and sufficient for the decision?
2. Has the outcome of the decision aligned with your expectations?
3. What could we have done differently to make the communication or analysis more effective?

This simple act transforms our communication from a one-off event into a learning opportunity.

With this framework at hand, we ever so slightly shifted our focus from pure analytics or data science towards decision intelligence (DI). DI is a relatively new field that combines data science, social science, and decision theory to improve organizational decision-making.

Expanding our skills

With these general guidelines at hand, we can now practice them. The following exercises can help you improve and eventually apply the principles, either individually or wholly, to your next professional communication. With the latter, you will receive feedback faster and more fitting to your professional context. But please do not be discouraged if the first iteration of feedback is something akin to "this is not how we used to do this." This may actually be the first step toward improving communication and, by extension, the data culture as a whole.

The following exercises, grouped into six sections, should be practiced consistently over months, not crammed in a single session. Regular repetition will lead to continuous growth.

Simplification

The first skill we will practice is keeping things simple. As Einstein said, "If you can't explain it simply, you don't understand it well enough." Simple does not automatically imply short; rather, it implies a reduction in complexity, which can be done in different ways, as you will see. Every exercise contains an expected time investment based on our experience.

The Four-Chunk Challenge (15 minutes)

Given our knowledge that we can hold only four pieces of information at any time, we will aim to provide exactly that. Let us take a look at a presentation, report, or analysis you recently created. For each slide, section, or the entire work, we will answer:

- What are the four or fewer key points we need the audience to retain?
- What did we include that exceeds this limit?
- For each excess item: Is this essential context, or are we including it because **we** find it interesting?

With the answers to these questions, we rewrite the initial piece and compare it to the original. Observe the process. What did it feel like to cut material? What fears come up? Common thoughts are "they won't understand without this" or "they'll think we didn't do enough work," but we should not take away our audience's right to form their own opinion.

Explain it like I am five (20 minutes)

This exercise or term is something of a trope or meme, especially on platforms like Reddit. But while it may sound ridiculous, it follows the sentiment of Einstein's quote. If we can explain our work to an unknowing and possibly naive audience, we can break it down to its simplest form. This does not imply that our day-to-day audience consists of 5-year-olds or that we should treat them like such.

Similar to the previous exercise, we will use recent data work, ideally a written paragraph, but anything works, and rework it. The goal is to create a short text that explains the content to our audience of five-year-olds. If you have not yet interacted with kids of this age, here are some rules to go by:

- No jargon or acronyms
- Assume only the most basic concepts are known
- No sentences longer than 15 words
- Use of concrete examples instead of abstractions
- No more than three minutes of reading time

After the rewrite is finished, we can compare it to the original. Let us consider the following questions:

- What did we need to understand more deeply to simplify it?
- Where did we discover our own confusion hiding behind complex language?
- Was anything lost in the translation?

Our experience is that simplifying work under this premise often leads to more convincing, memorable output. It is no surprise that one of the common use cases for AI chatbots is to break down complex topics along this basis. To provide an example, "Quantum physics is the set of rules for the tiniest pieces of the world, where things can be in many states at once, and where just looking at something can change what it is." We should check whether our writing has some accessibility.

One Sentence Only (10 minutes)

This exercise, or rather writing prompt, asks us to state our message in a single sentence. It can seem simple, but over-simplification is as unwanted as too much complexity. Before any meeting or presentation, or as part of creating our signal, we define the message as clearly as we can. The template for this is:

"If my audience remembers only one thing, it must be: _______________."

When we found it, we reviewed our prepared signal. Does everything support this sentence, or does anything distract from it? Anything unnecessary to us will be equally distracting for our audience.

We can use this way of focusing or clarity in most situations. Something to consider is how often we enter meetings without this clarity. What happens to our communication when we lack a single focal point?

Storytelling

As shown above, we aim to create a story, not just a still picture, with our signal. Humans are natural storytellers,[17] but can still fail when focusing on the facts. What makes a great story is often a question of personal taste, as you can tell by the range of human literature, from "50 Shades of Grey" to "War and Peace." Not everyone feels like an author, but with the following two exercises, we will see how easy it is to create convincing stories.

Find the Human (10 minutes)

Before we present any dataset, we write a one-paragraph story about one specific person affected by the pattern in our data. We make sure to give them a name, a context, and a challenge. Ideally, this person is a customer or an employee of our organization, not our CEO, with the problem of "not having enough numbers." As before, we will use a recent piece of data work to practice.

Template:

[Name] is a [role] who [situation]. When [the problem our data reveals], they experience [concrete consequence]. What they need is [what our insight points toward].

Something to consider after this exercise is how this person changed how we looked at our findings. Did their presence provide another perspective? Or did they provide more urgency to the topic?

Write a Data Story (25 minutes)

With the previous exercise, we created a protagonist but they still need an adventure to go on. There are common patterns for stories like the Hero's Journey,[18] but we will use fewer steps that also fit better with the context we are operating in. We take past data insights and restructure them using

---

17 Fisher, Walter R. "The narrative paradigm: An elaboration", 1985.

18 Campbell, J. "The Hero with a Thousand Faces", 1949.

narrative tension. Tension creates suspense by leaving us unsure of what happens next. This may sound counterintuitive in a professional context, but, as we will see, it breaks down into starting from an unclear or changing situation towards a solution. Surprisingly, we do not start with our key insight.

To create our story, we will use the following steps:

1. **Setup**. What was the world like before? What did we believe or assume?
2. **Tension**. What disrupted this? What's at stake? Why should we care now?
3. **Evidence**. What does the data reveal? (This is where our analysis lives.)
4. **Resolution**. What should we do? What becomes possible?
5. **Return**. Revisit the human from the previous exercise. What changes for them?

The goal is to write about a page of text. We do not care about style or poetic imagery; we just want to follow the structure as outlined. When we are done, we can reflect on the following questions:

- Why is it uncomfortable to create tension before showing data?
- What might our audience feel if we do?

The Opening Hook (15 minutes)

As recommended in many social media playbooks, a good opening line is equally helpful for us. We can consider it the headline of our signal. And like a good headline on a news site, it does not tell the full story, but enough to get us interested. For any recent data work, we write five hooks in the following formats:

- **A surprising fact**, for instance, "We're spending more on X than on our entire Y budget."
- **A question**, for instance, "What would it mean if we could cut this time in half?"
- **A contradiction**, for instance, "We assumed X. We were wrong."
- **A human moment**, for instance, "Last Tuesday, a customer called us in tears."
- **A bold claim**, for instance, "This one change could save us $X this year."

We can use this hook as the title for our presentation, our video, or our talk, or as the subject of the email we send out. The goal, as in journalism, is not to mislead but to frame the facts in a way that catches our audience's attention.

After we are done, we can ask ourselves:

- Which hook creates the most tension?
- Which makes our audience lean in?
- Which feels authentic to our voice?

The last one may lead us to expand our repertoire by deliberately choosing a hook outside our usual style.

Audience adaptation

We showed in the CLEAR framework that working with and for our audience is key to being convincing and memorable. Any audience has its own goals, context, and preferences. And we aim to meet them where they are. This includes two steps: understanding their needs and adapting to them. The following exercises provide the chance to do exactly that.

The Three Audiences (30 minutes)

We take one key insight from recent data work and write the opening paragraph for three different audiences:

- Petra, a (technical) peer who shares our expertise
- Sam, a senior executive with limited time and different priorities
- Richard, a skeptic who doubts our methodology or conclusions.

We need to consider what they would be most interested in. Petra likely wants to know how we approached the task, Sam wants to know how it affects the business, and Richard wants proof that we checked all angles. We could elaborate on these writing prompts, but adding specific examples from our organization will make them more relatable.

We compare the different paragraphs and consider the following questions:

- What stayed the same across all three? (This is our core message.)
- What changed? (This reveals our assumptions about what different audiences need.)
- Which version was hardest to write? Why?

The Pre-Mortem (15 minutes)

Let us imagine our upcoming presentation failed completely. The audience left confused, unconvinced, or disengaged. Instead of waiting until this happens and creating a post-mortem or retrospective analysis, we establish a pre-mortem to anticipate the causes. We write this short "autopsy" from the perspective of an audience member. We can use these starting points:

- *"The presentation lost me when..."*
- *"I didn't understand..."*
- *"I stopped caring because..."*
- *"I would have needed..."*

With this, we can revise our presentation to address what we just wrote. Additionally, we can ask ourselves how it felt to look at our work from an outside perspective.

The Curse of Knowledge (15 minutes)

The Curse of Knowledge[19] refers to the cognitive bias that everyone with specialized knowledge assumes that everybody else is equally versed in this field and shares their understanding. This assumption is often wrong and leads to miscommunication, either through the use of jargon or by omitting basic steps when explaining more complex issues.

While checking out some recent data work or preparing the next piece, we will get into the shoes of a new starter in our organization. We list every term, acronym, concept, or reference in our presentation that we learned after starting our current role. For each, we note:

- Would a smart person outside our field know this?
- If not, can we define it in a single sentence, or should we cut it?

This will lead to two things: a more approachable signal and awareness of our own cursedness. After the exercise, we can think of a time we were the newcomer in a room full of experts. What did it feel like when they used language you didn't understand? What did we wish they had done?

19Camerer, C.; Loewenstein, G.; Weber, M., "The Curse of Knowledge in Economic Settings: An Experimental Analysis", 1989.

Visual thinking

We know from personal experience that even the cleanest data or the most fantastic insight can fall flat if shown in the wrong format. But Visual communication is an established way of transmitting abstract ideas,[20] and that's what we often aim for: providing general guidance for decision makers. The following exercises focus on learning to translate concepts into imagery.

The Napkin (10 minutes)

A straightforward exercise: we take any piece of paper, possibly a napkin, and draw a single sketch representing our key message from some prior or current data work. It is important to do this by hand, not with any tool. We want to be completely free regarding form.

- What's the single visual relationship we try to show?
- Is it a comparison? A trend? A part-to-whole? A distribution?
- What's the simplest chart type that reveals this?

As always, there is the chance to reflect as soon as we find the core visual. How did sketching by hand change what we notice compared to jumping straight into Excel or Tableau?

Only 1 second (5 minutes)

For this exercise, we need a peer, regardless of whether they are in business, tech, or data. We pick a current chart or visual, or one previously created, and show it to them for one second. Ask them:

- What was the main message?
- What stood out first?

If their answer does not match our intent, our visual hierarchy needs work. Visual hierarchy describes the structure guiding viewers from the most important message to the supporting details. An example is the headlines and pictures in newspapers, which lead to the actual text. We can use color, size, or position to guide attention to what matters most.

---

20 See Ryan, Lindy "The Visual Imperative: Creating a Visual Culture of Data Discovery", 2016.

Fighting the Rainbow (15 minutes)

Alongside the principle of "minimal digital ink" (see earlier), we can also check our use of color. Often, we want to highlight every important aspect, or at least the ones that are important to us, of a visual or text. This can lead to a rainbow effect, an overly dramatic use of color that negates the intended effect of highlighting. For a recent visual or all of them, we check:

- How many colors did we use?
- What does each color *mean*? (If it doesn't mean anything, why is it there?)
- Could we reduce to two colors (one for emphasis, one for context)?
- Would this work in grayscale? (Test: print it black-and-white)
- Is our color choice accessible to colorblind viewers?

The rule of thumb should be to use color to highlight what matters, not to decorate. If available, our organization's style guide should support that notion. Or we can address it with the responsible people.

As reflection prompts, we can consider the following:

- When do we add color out of habit versus intention?
- What would ruthless color restraint look like in our work?

Numbers and Framing

If we are using raw numbers instead of visuals or numbers as part of text or visuals, we need to make sure they have the intended effect. It's about presentation. Consider the difference between the following two slides. They contain the same info, two values each, but shown in distinct ways (Figure 15).

Which will be more memorable or interesting? To which audience? Within the next exercises, we want to play a bit with these possibilities. As we know, a number without context is just noise.

Figure 15: The way you present numeric information makes a big difference.

The Flip (10 minutes)

We take some prior data work and pick the key statistic from it. And then we write or present this metric in two framings:

- **Positive frame:** What is gained, saved, or achieved?
- **Negative frame:** What is lost, at risk, or failing?

As examples:

- "90% success rate" versus "10% failure rate"
- "We retained 85% of customers" versus "We lost 15% of customers."

Again, those are the same numbers, but we can use them quite differently and provide a different framing. It is obvious that the decision regarding which framing to use is powerful and can be intentionally deceiving. So, within the exercises, we reflect upon the following questions:

- Which frame is more honest?
- Which is more motivating for our specific audience and goal?
- Are we using framing deliberately or accidentally?

Anchors (10 minutes)

The anchoring effect is a psychological phenomenon discovered by Tversky and Kahneman[21] that describes how reference points (*anchors*) influence one's judgments or decisions. The anchor is usually the first number we perceive. Any menu placing an expensive item first is using this mechanism, intentionally or unintentionally. This specific scenario is called "decoy effect", where all other options suddenly seem way more reasonable as they are not the expensive item.

For our exercise, we pick any recent data work and identify the first number our audience will see or hear in our presentation. Then we ask:

- Is this anchor helping or hurting our message?
- What number should the audience have in mind when evaluating our key insight?
- Can we restructure to introduce a more useful anchor first?

As an example, if we are proposing a $50,000 investment, starting with "Last year we lost $400,000 to this problem" makes $50,000 feel small. Starting with "Our typical project budget is $20,000" makes it feel large.

Comparisons (15 minutes)

Framing is often about comparing to others, for instance, benchmarking. And with the selection of the comparison, we can strongly influence the perception of any number. But that influence has to be wielded intentionally and in good faith. It is easy to choose a contrasting number that makes our results look more impressive than they actually are. Refer to the ethics section for guidance in that regard. We take a number from our work and write five different comparisons that give it meaning:

1. **Historical**, for instance, "Up 25% from last year."
2. **Goal-based**, for instance, "We're at 80% of our target."
3. **Peer comparison**, for instance, "Twice the industry average."
4. **Absolute scale**, for instance, "That's enough to fill 50 Olympic swimming pools."
5. **Per-unit**, for instance, "That's $12 per customer per month."

---

21 Tversky, A.; Kahneman, D. "Judgment under Uncertainty: Heuristics and Biases", 1974.

We will see how the context we provide changes the meaning and importance. This is the power of framing. We can consider which comparison makes the number most meaningful for our audience's decision?

Reflection

Reflection is an important part of critical thinking (see Chapter 4) and an equally powerful tool for improving our communication. In practice, it usually comes down to actively engaging with our past actions and their consequences, for us and others.

The Autopsy (20 minutes)

It is normal to be happy when the big presentation is finally done or the major report is sent out, but this is not where our work ends. We need to check what happens with our work. Within 24 hours after presenting, we journal on these questions:

- What questions did the audience ask? (These reveal what wasn't clear.)
- What objections came up? (These reveal what wasn't persuasive.)
- At what moment did we see engagement drop? (This reveals where I lost them.)
- What would we do differently with the same material?

With this, we get ever closer to understanding the needs of our audience and possibly the context in which they operate.

The (Weekly) Journal (15 minutes)

This is a general recommendation to start a work journal. There are many templates available, such as the bullet journal, gratitude journals, or simple grid setups, in both physical and digital forms. So there is space for us to try and experiment, finding our own style. The form does not matter as much as the consistent practice, investing those 15 minutes either daily or at least weekly.

A work journal serves as both a mirror and a map. It shows us where we are and helps us see where we have been. The act of writing forces clarity; vague feelings of "that presentation didn't go well" become specific observations like "I lost the room when I introduced the third data source without explaining why it mattered." This specificity is where growth lives.

Research on reflective practice, from Donald Schön's foundational work[22] onward, shows that professionals who regularly reflect on their experiences develop expertise faster than those who simply accumulate years on the job. A work journal also fights the forgetting curve; insights that feel obvious today vanish within weeks unless captured. Over months, patterns emerge that are invisible in the moment. We might notice that we consistently struggle with a particular type of stakeholder, or that our best ideas come on days when we start with a certain routine. Perhaps most importantly, a journal creates accountability to ourselves. It's easy to tell ourselves we will "communicate more clearly" or "be more strategic," but when we write down what we actually did and how it landed, self-deception becomes harder. The journal does not judge, but it does remember, and that memory becomes the foundation for deliberate improvement rather than hopeful repetition.

Checklist for Creating our Signal

- What concrete decision or behavior should this communication enable?
- Who is the receiver, and what do I know about their context and constraints?
- What is my core message in one sentence?
- Which three pieces of evidence are truly necessary to support it?
- How can I encode this message so it is easy to parse (structure, visuals, language)?
- Which channel gives it the best chance to be seen and understood?
- What noise should I expect (competing priorities, jargon, similar metrics) and how can I add redundancy or clarity to mitigate it?
- How will I gather feedback to see whether the message worked as intended?

Key takeaways

- We only control the sender side of communication.
- Data communication is often inherently noisy; let's not add to it.
- Set up CLEAR communication to make sure your message gets received.
- Communication can be improved with simple routines, like journaling.

22 Schön, D "The Reflective Practitioner", 1973.

Chapter 7

AI's Relationship to Critical Thinking, Communication, and Ethical Action

"[AI's] really an attempt to understand human intelligence and human cognition."

Sebastian Thrun

AI is a ubiquitous technology these days, so it feels right to address it in the context of critical thinking, communication, and ethics, especially given how much drama revolves around this tech. In essence, AI is an automated and lightweight reasoning system that enables faster iteration cycles across various processes, particularly those involving large amounts of data. If you see it this way, rather than some super-intelligent machine in the making, you are bound to benefit from it, all while avoiding the cognitive offloading that seems to be a trend nowadays when it comes to how we engage with AI systems.

In this chapter, we'll explore how it can be useful to us for our critical thinking and communication, be it as a research tool, as a tool for challenging our thinking, as a communication partner to practice with, as a way to help us get more ethical about action (see Figure 16 below), and how evaluating AI can also be a useful practice of all these skills. We'll wrap up the chapter with a use case/exercise. Through all this, we'll see that it's not necessarily an adversary, but it's not a tutor either. It's how we apply it that can make it useful.

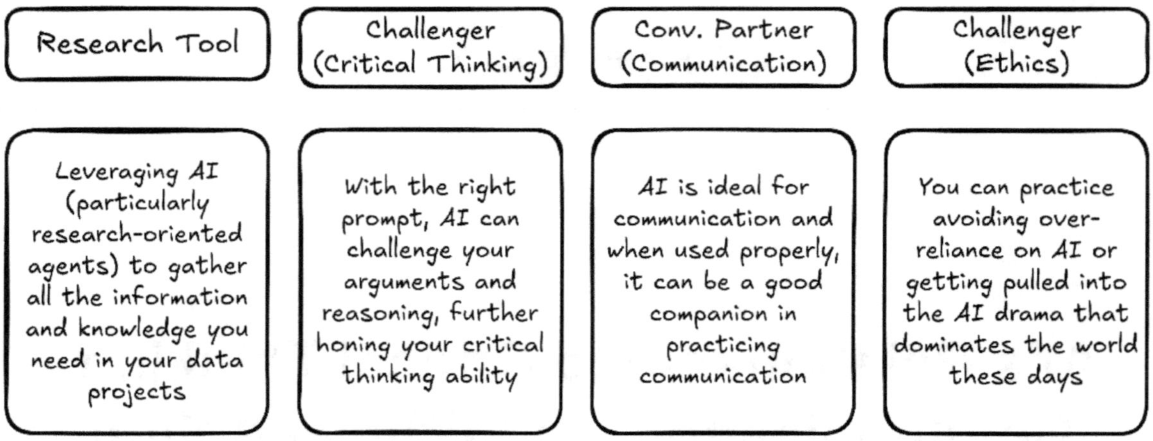

Figure 16: Key aspects of AI's role in critical thinking and communication.

AI as a sophisticated research tool

Many people use AI as a research tool, much like a search engine, but without any effort on our part. That's not always useful, though, as most AIs are trained on garbage data (for instance, Reddit posts and random blogs), so the quality of the results is questionable. On top of that, most AI systems hallucinate to some extent, making the waters murkier. However, critical thinking can turn all this into an asset as it thrives on such challenges. When the mind is disciplined and ready to challenge any new information it encounters, the outputs of an AI can be fertile ground for further developing critical thinking and benefiting from the research process.

Additionally, AI can provide you with ideas you wouldn't normally think of, broadening your understanding of a topic. Without accepting AI-generated ideas at face value, you can explore them and possibly find something of value in these areas that you would normally not venture into. Ideally, it would also provide you with some references (most modern AI systems do) that you can explore further and use in your work. This way, AI is like a useful librarian, an enhanced research assistant. The main project is still yours, along with the responsibility for it.

When it comes to practical matters, like coding, AI can yield semi-useful code, accelerating a data project. The code may not be optimal, but it may be a decent first draft. At the same time, it may help you come up with novel ways to frame a problem or a task programmatically, speeding things up. Naturally, you'll need to check whether the used libraries exist (another critical thinking opportunity) and that the code runs as expected. Perhaps this way you can spend more time on unit testing and overall quality control. If you are so inclined, you can even refine your programming skills by analyzing the AI-produced code and drawing useful takeaways from it.

Finally, AI can help you come up with creative ways to frame and express your ideas, fleshing out their core aspects. They may not be production-ready, but they can be good enough as a starting point. As long as it's not the end result, it can be useful, as you can use these expressions as stepping stones. In a way, AI can provide the building blocks of what you need to create. As long as the overall design and final version are yours (and this responsibility is coupled with an understanding of the inner workings of the programs involved), AI remains an auxiliary tool, and a useful one at that.

Although AI can be a valuable research tool, you are still in charge and (ideally) in control of your collaboration with AI. And most importantly, you are still responsible for the end result, especially if it's not as good as advertised. That's why fact-checking and verification of the information acquired through such a system are paramount. This is especially true for projects where the stakes are higher or where important decisions are made based on this research. Naturally, it would also be a good idea to be transparent about AI-assisted research, much as in certain multimedia content platforms, where AI-generated material needs to be explicitly identified. This way, additional attention (and critical thinking) would be encouraged for those who access this information.

Naturally, if everyone acted as proposed here, AI would be a useful resource rather than a problem or safety concern. To learn more about the safety aspect of AI, on both individual and collective levels, feel free to check out the book *AI Safety: Strategies for Ensuring Responsible, Ethical, and Reliable AI Systems* (Technics Publications).

AI as a tool for challenging your critical thinking

Even if AI is a great resource for research, it can be much more effective in the hands of someone like Chris Thomas, especially if that someone is eager to improve their critical thinking skills. This isn't about getting access to specialized AI systems but using the ones commonly available in a different way, directing your efforts into the how and the why rather than the what. Research shows that critical thinking wanes with excessive AI use, but it can also grow when AI is leveraged properly. Let's explore this possibility further.

Sparring with your critical mind is a time-consuming process, and most people don't have the time or motivation to help you with that. Fortunately, you can leverage AI for this, as it has infinite patience and is eager to help you. Granted that it will not be as sophisticated or challenging (in a good way) as a human being, but for starting off, it's a good option.

Additionally, AI can be prompted to challenge your thinking and help you identify potential blind spots. Just type or dictate your critical thinking process, upload any relevant diagrams you've made, and let it do its work. It may not find everything, but it is bound to identify the major ones and provide you with suggestions on how to address them. As a bonus, it can help you identify unnecessary assumptions and get a more objective perspective on the problem at hand. This is particularly important when dealing with complex problems that involve a lot of concepts and heuristics that you inevitably inherit once you undertake them, or when you have strong opinions or preconceptions on the topic at hand.

Moreover, AI can provide you with feedback on how you express your critical thoughts, helping you optimize their delivery. This may be more linked to communication, but it's still relevant in this context. AI may not fully understand your audience, but it knows its way around language and can help you express yourself more critically. A good use case for this is when your sentences are overloaded or ambiguous. AI can help you break them down into more palatable pieces and clarify their content. Ideally, in the process, it can also help you learn how to do this on your own.

Furthermore, AI can provide you with examples to help you cement your thought process. This will not only help your audience better follow your train of thought, but also you when dealing with complex problems or when you venture too far into the abstract space. As a bonus, through this process, the same AI system can also help you evaluate your conclusions and ground them in the real world. Reflection helps us connect with the big picture, but sometimes it's easier said than done. Fortunately, AI doesn't have this limitation, as it's always linked to a knowledge base that accurately describes the big picture, providing you with the necessary context.

Speaking of which, AI can aid the reflective part of the process, as it may offer a more objective perspective, helping you improve your perspective. This goes beyond providing you with the context needed to evaluate your critical thinking, but also enables you to think more objectively. This is a process that takes practice, of course, but if you use AI this way, it can be a powerful mechanism for developing a more objective perspective. Note that this is in no way a substitute for reflection or manual information processing. With experience, you'll be able to strike a healthy balance between AI feedback and relying on your own critical thinking process.

AI as a partner for communication practice

You probably don't need this book to tell you how AI is a great tool for communication, but we'll delve into this anyway, from a different angle: getting AI to help you become a better communicator. AI systems are agnostic in how you use them, and if you are keen on improving yourself, you are bound to use them as assets rather than shortcuts and automation hacks in your communications.

First of all, AI can be more than a passive respondent to your communication, as it's often used. Instead, it can be prompted to engage with you in a realistic way, a combination of support and skepticism. Note that most AI systems today tend to gravitate toward being supportive and engaging, since that is something their parent companies can profit from. However, whether someone wants to invite skepticism into a conversation is debatable, and AI systems tend to err on the side of caution in this regard. That's why they usually need to be asked explicitly to be skeptical, making conversation more challenging for you, especially if you are confident in the validity of your ideas.

Additionally, AI can be prompted to ask you clarification questions to help you refine your storytelling. Ideally, this is something you would do yourself, but it doesn't hurt to get some assistance in this area, at least in the beginning. One proven practice for refining storytelling is recording your communication and then playing it back to yourself after some time has passed, so you are more detached from it. It's even better if you have a transcript you can read and analyze. AI systems like Whisper (offline) and Riverside (online) can be very useful for transcription.

Moreover, AI can help you summarize your key points more effectively, delivering a more focused and coherent story. This is the case where you don't already have a structure with the key points clearly defined, of course. However, many people shy away from the idea of mind maps and planning in general, or they get so sidetracked by the storytelling that they may end up going into tangents or making points in an impromptu fashion. This is normal, especially if storytelling is new to you, and AI-based summarization can be very useful in that regard. Alternatively, it can serve as a sanity check to ensure your end result aligns with the original plan for your story.

What's more, AI can help you optimize your communication style and fix linguistic errors or spot ambiguity in your language. This is particularly useful if you are working with a language other than your native tongue or engaging with new terminology. It's a delicate balance between comprehensiveness and comprehensibility, something few have been taught. Although AI is by no means the best teacher, it can still be a useful sounding board that can enable you to refine your skills to embody this balance more. Ideally, you'll use this tool in tandem with feedback from people, particularly those akin to your target audience.

Furthermore, AI can provide you with suggestions as to how you can express the same ideas in a way more suitable for your target audience. Note the suggestions part of this strategy. The AI may not know your target audience, but if you don't know it well either, this approach may be helpful. Regardless, expressing an idea in different ways may help you understand it better and hone your mental flexibility, so it's definitely good practice. At one point, however, you'll need to test your expression abilities on the stage, even if it's with a small group of people. And if you really must have additional feedback, use AI to analyze the transcript of such a practice.

Finally, AI can help you refine your arguments by "attacking" them with probing questions to assess their solidity. This may be more linked to critical thinking, but it's still useful for communication practice. The fact that AI is generally benign (at least when it's not threatened) helps you disassociate the attack from any feelings of insecurity or general unease. This can help you view arguments for what they are and gradually improve them. At the end of the day, the only real enemies in communication endeavors are ignorance, misunderstanding, and presumption. If AI can help you guard against them, it can be a useful ally in your betterment efforts.

AI as a way to challenge you into acting ethically

We talked about ethics and action stemming from it in other parts of the book, but what does AI have to do with it? Well, it is a crucial factor, much like weights in physical exercise, that strengthens your muscles; AI can strengthen your ethical prowess. AI ethics is an enormous topic that more and more people are getting into, even if they don't actively tackle it.

For starters, AI can help you make ethics more practical by providing examples and potential scenarios arising from its misuse. These involve scenarios that you may not know about or consider without additional information. However, as they have been talked about in various corners of the web, the AI systems are bound to know about them and inform you. The challenge begins when you ponder this information and apply some ethical judgment. Ideally, you'd go beyond the facts and dilemmas the AI will pose for you and apply some exploration of your own on this topic. Even if your ideas aren't entirely original, it's better than being passive.

What's more, AI can act as a true/false detector for soundbites and media messages from AI figureheads, identifying the agenda behind the words used and the ethical issues. This can shield you to some extent from the AI-driven drama that dominates the world today. That's not to say that the whole matter doesn't warrant close attention, but focusing too much on the carefully crafted content around it isn't always productive. A more level-headed approach to the AI issue is warranted, especially given the latest developments and societal implications of this technology.

Additionally, AI can suggest ethical actions tailored to your situation. Naturally, you shouldn't follow these suggestions blindly, but use them as options to consider and explore further. Perhaps the AI can come up with ideas you hadn't thought about. Naturally, the more information you give it about your situation and the limitations involved, the better the suggestions will be. In cases like these, it's best to opt for a Retrieval Augmented Generation (RAG) system and use multiple AI models to ensure more reliable outputs and greater diversity overall. Keeping other stakeholders in the loop is also important here since it's unlikely you'll be taking action on your own. Remember that if things don't go as planned, you'll be the one held responsible, not the AI.

Furthermore, AI can be a powerful feedback mechanism for your ethics by helping you evaluate and refine your ideas on the topic and how you apply them. Again, it's best to be as detailed as possible in your description of the situation, including any relevant documents you have at your disposal. The more context the AI has, the more likely it is for it to give you useful feedback. Here, it's also crucial that you can follow along and understand the refinement process step by step. It's not enough for the AI to yield some good outputs; it's as important, or even more important, to help you understand why these outputs are better versions of your original inputs and why the suggested refinements need to take place.

Finally, through the demystification of AI's capabilities and its value-adds, you can learn to depend on it less. This may sound like an oxymoron after all the stuff we've talked about, but if you think about it, it makes sense. The key here is to understand that AI plays a supporting role in your ethical action journey. By interacting with it, you may gain some value, but it is likely to be mostly present at the beginning. Ideally, you'll grow beyond it and learn to rely more on your abilities than on AI systems. This is akin to the critical thinking and communication frameworks, which are helpful mainly at the beginning.

Beyond all that, ethics has a special relationship with AI, as we alluded to throughout this book. We need to view it as a direct application of ethics and take proper (ethical) action in relation to it, while we still have this option. With AI systems often getting out of hand and acting in ways we haven't foreseen, it's time to step back and assess whether this tool is truly an asset and how we can ensure it remains valuable. This is a very nuanced matter and cannot be done justice in a single section of a book.

AI evaluation as an application of critical thinking and communication

AI evaluation is a practical field that emerged as more AI systems became available to the public. It involves rating different systems based on responses to everyday problems, particularly in terms of reliability, robustness, fairness, responsibility, and other factors such as speed and cost. It is a complex field that encompasses the evaluation of non-AI tools, including most machine learning systems. Although in its simplest form, it's appealing mostly to PMs and AI consultants, AI evaluation is something everyone needs to do, to the extent they know how. Even if you don't understand the various specialized metrics used to assess an AI model, you can still tell, to some extent, if its output is useful and meaningful, or if it's mimicking the average Reddit user. If you don't do it, it's a bit naive to expect the experts to take interest in your particular AI system, especially if it's something customized like a RAG based on your organization's sensitive data.

Naturally, AI evaluation can incorporate critical thinking and communication to a large extent, as it's a process based on objective judgment and effective expression of relevant findings. Even if you are not equipped with the specialized know-how (which is actually quite accessible nowadays), you can still evaluate an AI system quite well and let all the stakeholders know what they need to know about it if you apply the frameworks put forward in this book. The key thing is to be open-minded and unaffected by the marketing aspects of the AI systems. Instead, you can focus on the custom benchmarks you put together to evaluate the system, exploring how useful they are in your specific use cases.

It's important to remember that you don't need a certificate to do an AI evaluation. It's a relatively new field, and while certifications are useful, they're not a strict requirement. In fact, the main things you need are some general understanding of how ML/AI systems operate, a bit of prompt engineering, and a lot of patience. Of course, having a strong sense of critical thinking and ethics can go a long way in doing a good job at it. The latter is also key, as it helps you evaluate the system's subtler aspects, such as biases, fairness, alignment, and privacy. Even if you don't get all of these verticals fully, you can still have a sense of whether the AI has an objective view of the world, or if it's keen to parrot the prejudices of those who developed it, or exploit your data.

We would be amiss if we didn't mention the role of interdisciplinary collaboration in AI evaluation. For large-scale evaluations in particular, diverse teams from different areas need to come together (for instance, ethics committees, lawyers, SMEs, and even end-user reps). To make this collaboration feasible, extensive communication would be required. This not only ensures the different teams aren't siloed, but also makes the whole collaboration more efficient and able to get to the heart of the matter. If you were to be involved in such a collaboration, your communication skills could be one of the decisive factors of its success, a true force multiplier.

Given how AI systems constantly evolve, it's important to keep in mind that AI evaluation should follow the same rhythm and be part of a continuous improvement framework (for instance, Total Quality Management). It's tempting to make a one-off evaluation and call it a day, but what good would that do? To ensure a consistent standard of quality in AI systems, we need iterative evaluation. Ideally, this would involve feedback loops from the users and any other stakeholders, focusing on real-world scenarios. If you were to be involved in evaluating AI, you'd have plenty of opportunities to apply critical thinking, particularly when it comes to questioning assumptions about the AI system and analyzing all the relevant facts.

AI evaluation is also particularly meaningful, especially as more and more AI options are made available. This makes it a useful, perhaps even necessary, application. In fact, it can even be considered low-hanging fruit, much as prompt engineering was a couple of years ago. AI evaluation may not be valued as much, for reasons that may be quite apparent once you get into it, but it's key for making good choices when it comes to which AI systems to make part of your workflow or deploy in your organization. It is by far one of the most important decisions you can make in the long run. Just as choosing a particular operating system for your computer can impact your digital life for years to come, choosing an AI system may have a similar impact. Fortunately, it's a bit easier to switch to a different AI than to switch an operating system, especially if you are motivated by ethical principles.

Case study

For this case study, let's explore a fictitious scenario based on a retail chain called ValueMart. This organization, comprising 200 stores and five million loyalty members, leverages AI to offer personalized discounts. The model was trained on data based on customer purchase history, browsing behavior, and demographics. As one would expect, the goal was to maximize revenue through the use of exclusive offers targeted at high-spending customers. Analytics showed that 62% of the revenue would come from this minority class of shoppers. The decision seemed like a no-brainer and was acted on by the end of the workday.

What went wrong?

The problem that ensued was two-fold. First, there was a clear bias toward high spenders, leaving all other customers feeling undervalued and particularly unfair to loyal, budget-conscious shoppers, while exploiting vulnerable groups who were likely to overspend because of these discount incentives. Then there was also the issue of short-term thinking, which jeopardized brand trust and significantly reduced customer lifetime value, as they opted for other retailers that didn't treat them like second-class citizens.

The problem at hand wasn't just a qualitative one. It was reflected in specific metrics and other measurable matters. For instance, despite the modest 8% increase in revenue in the first quarter, customer satisfaction dropped by an unprecedented 12%, while, unsurprisingly, 5% of customers churned due to budget constraints. The customer service department was flooded with complaints like "I've shopped here for 10 years, but I never get the good coupons. Meanwhile, my neighbor, who spends twice as much, gets 20% off every week. It feels like you're punishing me for being careful with my money!" Clearly, you don't need an AI to tell you that this is really bad and that the problem is only going to get worse if left unaddressed!

How critical thinking, communication, and ethics saved the day

To resolve this problem, ValueMart engaged a consultant. Upon analyzing the available information, they deduced that the problem stemmed from reinforced inequality and trust erosion, driven by biases in the AI system's design. To address these issues, the consultant proposed a new strategy that is guided by ethical guardrails and well-thought-out processes around them, involving meaningful communication with everyone involved.

First and foremost, critical thinking entered the scene, and all the AI's assumptions had to be questioned. Inquiries like "What does 'valuable customer' really mean? Is it just spend, or also loyalty and potential?" and "How might this system exploit vulnerable groups?" were put forward and discussed. The consultant then proposed the use of a *bias audit checklist* to help identify and address biases in the system, particularly those related to demographics and other sensitive forms of segmentation of the customer base. This was made into a poster, too, to ensure that similar problems are kept at bay by proactively addressing biases in the future.

Following this, the ethical guardrails came into play through the discussion and definition of what constitutes *value* in a ValueMart customer. From the analysis that followed, three factors were identified and clearly defined within the organization's marketing terminology: loyalty, fairness, and potential. As fairness is the broadest of them, it was decided to create a metric to measure it, the *fairness-loyalty score*. This involved summarizing how discounts were distributed across customers' income brackets and how long they've been shopping at ValueMart. Plans for a new metric for a customer's potential were also put forward once the first one was validated and additional data became available.

For communicating the new strategy, a multi-tiered approach was used. Namely, for executives, the message was more high-level and relevant to their leadership role: "We're not just optimizing for revenue. We're building long-term trust and loyalty." For the marketing team, the message was more geared to their work: "Let's frame this as *rewards for loyalty, not just spending*." For the data professionals, the message was tailored to what's most relevant to their field: "Let's turn this situation into an opportunity to learn more from the data at hand and explore new heuristics to access the signals in it." Finally, for the customers, the message, in the form of a transparent email explaining the changes, was as follows: "We're updating our discounts to reward all loyal shoppers, not just big spenders. You are all valued, and we appreciate your business."

Key lessons

From this case study, we can derive various lessons to apply to how we deal with similar situations. For example, we can deduce the following:

- **Human-AI Collaboration**. AI can suggest actions and predict useful information, but humans must set ethical guardrails and design its functionality accordingly.
- **Win-Win Outcomes**. Critical thinking helps teams align AI with business and social goals. The aim is to move forward and make everyone feel content, not to make a quick buck.
- **Metrics Matter**. Track not just revenue but also fairness and customer satisfaction. Although too many metrics can be confusing, it's better to deal with them than to rely on a single metric, which is bound to be biased.
- **Ethics Drive Long-Term Profits**. Fairness isn't just moral but also good for business. Trust leads to higher retention and spending, along with the potential for long-term growth.

- **Communication Bridges the Gap.** Explaining changes to customers and stakeholders builds trust and alignment across all the stakeholders, and gradually with the AI itself.

Key takeaways

- AI as a research tool offers a low-effort way to generate ideas, drafts, and creative frameworks, but its outputs, often based on inconsistent data and prone to hallucination, require rigorous critical thinking, fact-checking, and verification; when used responsibly, it can enhance research, spark creativity, and accelerate projects, though ultimate responsibility for accuracy and quality remains with you, as a user.
- AI can be a powerful tool for developing and refining critical thinking, when used intentionally: While excessive reliance on AI may dull critical thinking, leveraging it as a patient, objective sparring partner (for instance, challenging assumptions, identifying blind spots, optimizing communication, providing real-world examples, and aiding reflection) can significantly enhance critical thinking skills, especially for those willing to focus on the "how" and "why" rather than just the "what."
- AI can be a proactive partner in honing communication skills if used intentionally. Beyond passive responses, AI can act as a supportive yet skeptical sparring partner, refine storytelling through clarification questions, summarize key points for coherence, optimize language and style (especially for non-native speakers), tailor messaging for different audiences, and stress-test arguments. This can help users build resilience, clarity, and adaptability in communication, while encouraging self-reflection and real-world practice.
- AI can act as a dynamic tool for strengthening ethical reasoning by providing practical examples, detecting biases in media, suggesting tailored ethical actions, offering feedback for refinement, and ultimately helping users internalize ethical judgment, serving as a supplementary guide that users should grow beyond over time.
- Ethics in AI is a critical matter that deserves proper attention. Two ways it can be tackled are ethical design of AI systems and AI evaluation.

- AI evaluation is a practical, interdisciplinary field that anyone, regardless of expertise, can and should engage in, focusing on assessing AI systems (and related tools) for reliability, fairness, ethics, and real-world usefulness through critical thinking, custom benchmarks, and continuous, collaborative feedback, rather than relying solely on certifications or marketing claims.
- Ethical guardrails and human oversight must guide AI systems to avoid reinforcing biases; aligning AI with both business and social goals (prioritizing fairness, loyalty, and transparency) builds long-term trust, customer satisfaction, and sustainable profits, while clear communication ensures alignment across all stakeholders.

Conclusion

"The capacity to innovate – the ability to solve problems creatively or bring new possibilities to life – and skills like critical thinking, communication, and collaboration are far more important than academic knowledge."

Tony Wagner

Based on the scenarios we discussed throughout this book, it's clear that critical thinking is an extremely useful trait in data work. However, it goes beyond this, making for a more level-headed life overall. In particular, it enables a more evergreen strategy in a variety of ventures, particularly those that involve complex situations where conventional reasoning and intuition don't suffice. In our fast-paced world, making sense of anything without critical thinking is nearly impossible. The same applies to communication and ethics, as we'll look at again later on.

Critical thinking helps us become better people, too. It elevates our understanding of the world, helping us navigate its nuances and discover new ways to contribute constructively. It's no wonder it's taught in various educational institutions, though not always effectively or engagingly. Beyond helping us solve quantitative problems, it's also an essential life skill that enables us to tackle difficult situations and organize our lives accordingly.

Similarly, communication is a powerful trait that extends beyond data-related matters. It bridges gaps among people and serves as a catalyst for diverse collaborations and creative projects. In a world where silos are more present than ever (even if they are not as obvious), a society fragmented by divisive views and ideologies, it's hard to fathom how anyone can navigate life without this invaluable ability. Undoubtedly, AI can alleviate some issues, and chatbots are becoming increasingly accommodating, but it's unlikely that it will ever replace the need for human-to-human communication.

Additionally, communication enables us to become better people and optimize our feedback processes across different activities. Everyone needs feedback, even if they don't realize it. Being able to provide it in a way that is beneficial and respectful is an art, however, which falls under the communication umbrella. Whether it's verbal or written, it has the potential to refine a product, service, project, and organization, so why not make the most of this opportunity?

As for ethics, it can help us become more long-term thinkers and actors, ensuring our data projects remain relevant in the years to come. In a time when AI agents are changing the way data is used and analyzed, ethical action is one of the things that sets us apart and makes us more relevant. As AI systems become more complex and more integrated into our lives, ethics can help keep them aligned with our values and useful tools. Otherwise, it can degrade into a dystopian threat that may cause all kinds of issues in our individual lives and our society in general. Ethical action, in that sense, is an essential part of our role and a crucial differentiator for a successful data-driven organization.

Put together, the trifecta of critical thinking, communication, and ethical action is a powerful skillset that can help us grow and enable growth in others. Not every problem can be turned into a data problem (even if some quantification is usually possible). Still, every problem we reason about and express linguistically can be tackled with critical thinking, communication, and ethics when properly leveraged. And if you think about them in relation to science, they are in essence a version of the scientific method, our greatest weapon against ignorance and prejudice, in the data world.

With everything in the tech world changing so rapidly in the past few years, from blockchain to quantum computing to AI, it seems that making predictions like this is futile. However, no matter what kinds of automations come about through these technologies, critical thinking, communication, and ethics are bound to remain and probably become even more relevant. Decision-making isn't going to just disappear, even if it is bound to become more data-driven. As long as decisions are to be made, critical thinking will be necessary to make that possible, while communication will be essential to give them traction and ethics to keep them aligned with our principles and values.

Even if AI advances as its more optimistic predictions suggest, we will still need to be able to make sense of its outputs (critical thinking) and communicate with everyone involved. AI systems are impressive, but they are not panaceas. When an AI inevitably breaks or needs fine-tuning, it's doubtful that individuals without critical thinking or communication skills would be able to offer much! As AI becomes smarter, it's doubtful that we'll be able to follow their processes without getting closely involved in their troubleshooting and alignment efforts.

Additionally, as AI becomes increasingly difficult to keep safe, critical thinking will continue to play a key role. This can be done by providing guardrails for it and in helping each of us find the best way to leverage it constructively. Just as with any technology, things don't go as planned, and safety gradually becomes a greater concern. If we look at the automobile industry, for example, it's clear that among the most prominent innovations in cars over the past few years were safety-related upgrades, such as ABS, cruise control, and parking cameras. Critical thinking may be the key tool necessary to make similar upgrades to the intelligence vehicles of the world's cyber roads.

Furthermore, as AI becomes more ubiquitous, communication is bound to be key for ensuring everyone is heard, not just responded to by a chatbot. This is especially true when new ideas are needed, beyond the synthesis of existing ones that AI can readily provide. Just like the car hasn't made trekking and cycling obsolete (in many urban environments, it has actually made cycling more pronounced), AI's effect on the social aspects of the world will likely be equally nuanced. Naturally, AI stakeholders would argue differently as they have their interests to protect. However, the reality is that people still enjoy talking with others and brainstorming ideas together, even with intelligent machines around. For example, when AI models fail (like the infamous case of a hiring algorithm favoring male candidates we explored earlier in the book), critical thinking is required to identify biases, and communication is essential to align stakeholders on corrective actions.

Finally, as AI systems become more complex and risky, ethics can help us manage them more effectively and ensure they are better aligned with our values, not just in how we use them, but also in how we design them or upgrade them. AI was always meant to be a tool, a particularly good one, too. Ethics can ensure that it also remains a safe and reliable one in the foreseeable future.

As we saw throughout the book, ethical action is a form of collaboration that is both fair and productive, combining critical thinking and communication harmoniously. It involves aligning all stakeholder groups (e.g., creators, administrators, and users) and establishing a shared frame of reference anchored in common values. Ethical action is essential to the effective application of critical thinking and communication. It's also extremely difficult to have ethical action without these abilities coming into play. That's why, after cultivating them, the next logical step is to coordinate and align them through ethics. By taking action based on sound reasoning (critical thinking) and proper communication, we can bring out the best in all of us and push the envelope on every project we undertake. With ethical action driving us, we are in no shortage of incentives, while we don't need to rely on motivation as much. It's a kind of inspiration that drives us from within, urging us to put in the extra work to pay attention to the details and ensure that every aspect of a data project or initiative is aligned with the final aim, benefiting everyone. It's what helps us stay grounded in reality while exploring possibilities going beyond spreadsheets and Gannt charts.

Ethical action takes the principles and values we aspire to and makes them a reality, making both our critical thinking and communication efforts meaningful and more effective. This enables them to be useful tools and powerful means of making things happen, rather than causes in and of themselves. No one is going to criticize you for being an excellent critical thinker or a charismatic communicator.

Ethical action enables us to innovate and avoid the stagnation that inevitable overreliance on technology brings. Sure, we can play it safe and ruminate constructively with AI, but eventually we'll lose steam. True innovation often goes beyond combining known parts to create a new design. That's what separates great artists from the just good ones. And with the world's data as our palette, we have no excuse for not doing something great. For this to be feasible, however, we need to employ our own intelligence and ethical action rather than artificial ones and comfortable actions. We need to take a chance and try something novel, even if it's not what ChatGPT suggests or encourages at first.

Ethical action is not just a philosophical ideal,
but a practical foundation for building a resilient organizational culture.

There are different ways to implement these abilities in a workforce. Still, the best way to make them a mid- and long-term reality is to embed them in the organization's culture. Ideally, a culture would be founded upon values and principles that can serve as a good starting point for imbuing it with these traits. As this is not usually possible, especially for older organizations, there needs to be a strategy to integrate them into the culture. Naturally, this would align with the organization's data strategy as well. In practice, incorporating these qualities ought to start with the C-level leadership team (leadership and vision). The executives will need to lead by example and apply critical thinking, communication, and ethical action in their day-to-day, especially in the decisions that everyone else has access to. The vision for the organization needs to reflect that. Instead of just mimicking other, more successful or more popular organizations, the organization needs to adopt an independent approach to its mission, grounded in a critical analysis of facts and data, organic communication with all stakeholders, and an ethical mindset.

To make these qualities part of the data culture, we can foster data literacy and skills, enable better data accessibility, foster better decision making, promote better collaboration and community, promote responsible and ethical use of data, invest in proper technology and infrastructure, and finally, work on developing the right cultural mindset (focusing on critical thinking, communication, and ethics) in particular (see Figure 17).

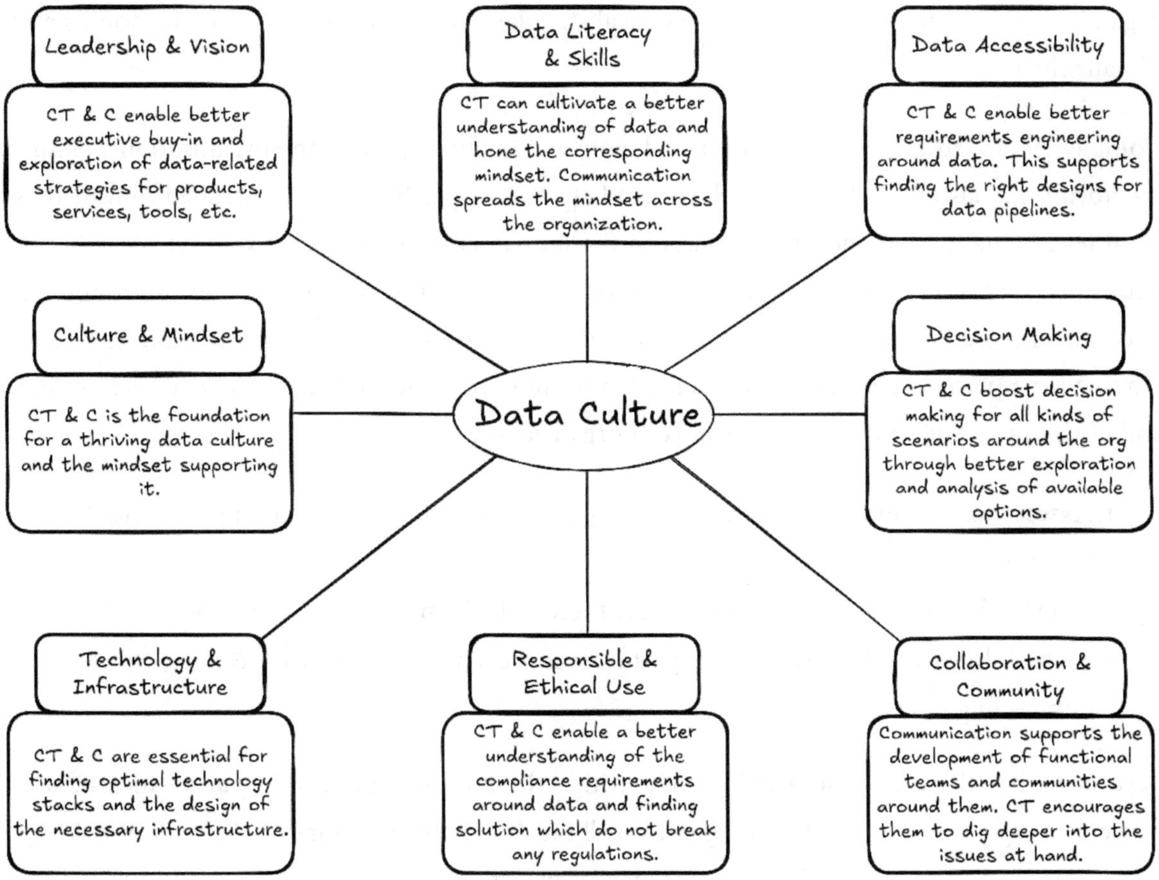

Figure 17: Critical thinking and communication, and their incorporation in an organization's data culture.

In parallel with these qualities embedded in the data culture, ethical action can serve as the glue that binds them together within the organization's vision. In terms of data, this can take the form of respect for the people, revision of the models, responsibility of each data worker, and reputation management, as we saw in Chapter 5. Companies like Patagonia, for example, have embedded ethical action into their culture by prioritizing environmental responsibility, thereby strengthening both their brand and employee engagement. Why not do something similar with ethical actions in other, more data-related verticals of the organization's function?

Naturally, any new initiative in the organization can be a great opportunity to push these qualities and inspire its members to adopt them. Rather than creating separate initiatives, embed these traits into every initiative, project, and task. That's the best way for them to become a true part of the organization's culture instead of just some idealistic plan that will be forgotten a few months after it's launched.

Complementary to all these tactics for making these qualities part of the organization's culture, mentoring can also be of help. Namely, it can help tackle specific challenges related to how these qualities are manifested and grown, on both the individual and the collective level. Whether it's performed within the organization or by leveraging external mentors, it can have a pronounced effect on the organization's culture, especially in the initial stages of transformation. If you are looking for a place to start, here is a rough plan for how you can implement these ideas right here and now, to start building this culture in your organization:

1. **Assess.** Survey your team on current strengths and gaps in critical thinking, communication, and ethical action.
2. **Model.** Have leaders visibly demonstrate these traits in meetings and decision-making.
3. **Embed.** Integrate these values into performance reviews, project retrospectives, and onboarding.

Beyond all that, there are other ways to make critical thinking, communication, and ethical action part of the organization's DNA, freeing it from all the drama that surrounds data work. We don't have all the answers, nor would sharing more information on this matter help. As AI and automation reshape our world, the organizations that thrive will be those that harness the power of critical thinking, communication, and ethical action. Will your organization embrace this opportunity to evolve? What's one small change you can make this week to foster critical thinking or ethical action in your team?

In a world drowning in artificial intelligence and noise, the ability to think critically, communicate clearly, and act ethically is not just an advantage but the very essence of our humanity.

Index

www.ingramcontent.com/pod-product-compliance
Lightning Source LLC
LaVergne TN
LVHW060041210926
848481LV00013B/3923
9798898160852